Making the Link
Teacher Professional Development on the Internet

Ron Owston

HEINEMANN
Portsmouth, NH

HEINEMANN
A division of Reed Elsevier Inc.
361 Hanover Street
Portsmouth, NH 03801-3912

Offices and agents throughout the world

The author and publisher thank those who generously gave permission to reprint borrowed material:

Figures 3–1, 3–2, 3–3, 3–4, 3–5, 3–6, 3–7, 3–8, 7–1, and 7–2 used with permission of Netscape Communications Corporation. Netscape Communications Corporation has not authorized, sponsored, or endorsed, or approved this publication and is not responsible for its content. Netscape and the Netscape Communications Corporate Logos, are trademarks and trade names of Netscape Communications Corporation. All other product names and/or logos are trademarks of their respective owners.

Figure 6–1 reproduced with the permission of Liszt.

Figures 10–1 and 10–2 reproduced with the permission of Digital Equipment Corporation. AltaVista and the AltaVista logo and the Digital logo are trademarks of Digital Equipment Corporation.

Figures 10–3, 10–4, and 10–5 reproduced with the permission of Yahoo! Inc. Copyright 1994–96 Yahoo! Inc. All Rights Reserved.

Figures 11–1, 11–2, 11–3, 11–4, 11–5, and 11–6 reproduced with the permission of the University of Texas at Austin General Libraries website.

Figures 11–7 and 11–8 reproduced with the permission of AskERIC. Http://ericir.syr.edu.

Figures 12–3 and 12–4 reprinted with permission from CNET, Inc. Copyright 1995–97. www.cnet.com. CNET, Inc. has not authorized, sponsored, endorsed, or approved this publication and is not responsible for its content.

Figures 12–7, 12–8, 12–9, and 12–10 reproduced with the permission of Deja News.

Be sure to visit *Making the Link*'s Web site, *http://www.edu.yorku.ca/MTL,* where you'll find links to all Web sites referenced in the text, updates, resource links, and a professional-development discussion forum.

Library of Congress Cataloging-in-Publication Data
Owston, Ronald Davis, 1945-
     Making the link : teacher professional development on the Internet
 / Ron Owston.
          p.   cm.
     Includes bibliographical references and index.
     ISBN 0-325-00077-8
     1. Teachers—In-service training.   2. Internet (Computer network)
 in education.   3. Education—Computer network resources.   I. Title.
     LB1731.O97   1998
     370'.71'5—dc21   97-50314
                                                       CIP

Editor: Victoria Merecki
Production: Melissa L. Inglis
Cover design: Gary Ragaglia/Metro Design
Manufacturing: Louise Richardson

Printed in the United States of America on acid-free paper
02 01 00 99 98 RRD 1 2 3 4 5 6 7 8 9

Contents

Acknowledgments

Most of us, when first introduced to the Internet, go through the wildly exciting stage of surfing the Net, discovering interesting tidbits of information, visiting home pages of our favorite Hollywood stars, searching for our family name, checking out sites that we see advertised on television, gleaning ideas for using in our classrooms. After a while, though, the novelty wears off and we ask the question "Is that all there is?" The answer to this question is an emphatic "No!" *Making the Link* attempts to help teachers take the "next step" with the Internet—to use it as a tool for their personal professional growth.

The genesis of the book arose from conversations with Leigh Peake, then acquisitions editor at Heinemann. Leigh's vision was to create a book that was not just another how-to-do-it guide to the Internet for teachers. She encouraged me to write a book that would inspire teachers to use the Internet for professional development by providing them with practical advice and ideas. To Leigh I owe my gratitude for her inspiration and confidence in me to rise to this challenge. Thanks are also due to Sandra Wilde, professor of education at Portland State University, former colleague, and friend, who introduced me to Leigh.

Much of the planning and early writing for the book occurred during a sabbatical year at the University of Texas at Austin. My appreciation goes to Nolan Estes, L. D. Haskew Centennial Professor of Education, who encouraged me to spend the year in Austin, and who helped me gain access to the university's resources and facilities, without which the project would not have been possible.

As the project evolved Victoria Merecki inherited editorial responsibility at Heinemann from Leigh Peake. Coming into the project midstream was undoubtedly a challenge, however Victoria rose to the occasion admirably. She handled the tough editorial decisions, which are inevitably part of any project, with aplomb. Her critical editorial eye and expertise shaped my manuscript into the text you are now reading. Thank you, Victoria, for your guidance and editorial suggestions.

Many others at Heinemann had a hand in seeing this project through to completion: Melissa Inglis, for production; Gary Ragaglia, for the cover design; and Louise Richardson, for manufacturing. To all of you, I express my appreciation.

The teachers who contributed their stories to this book deserve special thanks too. Although I had only met most of them online, their willingness to trust me and contribute their experiences is sincerely appreciated. I also want to thank Don Tapscott, who in his book *The Digital Economy* drew my attention to the poignant quote from Robertson Davies with which I begin the introduction.

Finally, a debt of gratitude goes to my wife, Anke, whose enthusiasm for the project motivated me to keep plodding ahead. She deserves thanks too for her critical reading and suggestions during the early stages of the manuscript. Without her encouragement and support, I may never have completed this book.

Introduction:
Professional Development and the Internet

I'm always trying to move on to something else. If possible, I want to be less stupid. Of course, the less stupid you are, the more you realize just how stupid you really are! If you give up the struggle, you give up life. You've got to be perpetually taking in what's happening. The world I live in is so much different from the world in which I was born that if I didn't pay attention, I'd be a fossil. — Author Robertson Davies, at age 80

All of us who teach have memories of professional-development sessions we've attended. Some were outstanding and rewarding experiences—others were ones we'd like to forget. I recall one workshop, in the early 1970s during my first year of high school teaching, in which I found myself lying on the gym floor with my teacher colleagues, "meditating" in small groups. According to the workshop facilitator, who had just flown in from California at great expense to the school district, we were supposed to be "getting in touch" with our inner consciousness to help us improve our teaching. Foremost on my mind, however, was how I would deal with a student I was meeting at noon who consistently refused to do his homework and acted up in class. And secondly, I was wondering why nobody told us to dress appropriately for the workshop, as I saw the women squirming uncomfortably on the floor, trying to keep their skirts below their knees, and the men all wearing jackets and ties.

What struck me at the time was how unrelated this workshop was to what I, as a first-year teacher, really needed. I desperately wanted help with managing my mathematics classes of thirty teenagers, who were more interested in who they were going to Friday's dance with than in how to solve quadratic equations. I'd rather have spent the morning talking to the other math teachers about problems I was having, sharing ideas on how to make math more relevant and engaging, and learning how they'd deal with the student I was seeing at noon. From the moans and groans during the workshop—and the buzz during the coffee break—other teachers were feeling much the same. We had no voice in the planning of the workshop. Apparently, the vice principal who organized it didn't either, because he was shocked and embarrassed by what the facilitator was having us do.

Now many years later, as a teacher educator, I find myself in the same position as the California consultant. From time to time I'm invited to lead a professional-development workshop or speak at a school district conference. When I look over the group I'm speaking to, I frequently wonder how relevant and useful what I'm saying is to them. Although they may leave the session excited and full of new ideas, for all but a few, reality probably sets in when they return to their classrooms. More immediate problems usually need to be tended to, such as teaching the day's language arts lesson to their class, a third of which is made up of students whose first language is not English, or preparing their students for an upcoming statewide proficiency test. Again, the teachers in attendance probably had little say in choosing me as the speaker, the topic of my session was not likely one that was a burning issue for them, and no doubt there were at least a half-dozen other kinds of more relevant professional-development activities they'd rather be engaged in than sitting listening to me.

Taking Charge of Your Professional Development

For most of the twentieth century, the kind of professional-development experience I've just described has dominated teaching. I'll call it the *delivery mode* of professional development, because the experience is seen as something that is "delivered" to teachers. Typically, in the delivery mode, teachers attend brief one-shot workshops or conferences led by authorities in the topic, or they might attend a course given by a university or school district taught by an expert in the field. Underlying the delivery mode of professional development is the assumption that the expert's knowledge is more valid than yours, as an individual teacher; that you are not really capable of growing professionally on your own; and that outsiders generally know better what kind of professional development you need.

While there will always be a role for this type of instruction, for example to inform you about new programs and curriculum, to bring you up to date on the latest developments in a particular field, and to inspire, motivate, and boost your morale, its usefulness is limited. Professional development should be a continuous, sustained process centered around the problems you face in your classroom. It must build upon your knowledge and understanding of children and the dynamics of your classroom. Moreover, professional development must be tailored to suit your background, experiences, needs, and aspirations, as a "one size fits all" approach is not a productive use of your time. The only way for this to happen is for you to take a proactive role in your professional development, to take charge in planning and managing the way you grow professionally. It is ironic that for decades we have encouraged children to become independent learners, to pursue their own interests, and to "construct" their own understandings and interpretations, *yet few suggest that teachers be given this opportunity too*!

Taking control of your professional development is not easy, particularly if you are used to relying on others to let you know about new practices and ideas or advances in your subject areas. Taking control also requires commitment, planning, and time. But the rewards you will derive from the effort will be ample. Most significant is that your professional-development path will be one that you choose, not one that others say is best for you. You can build a path that reflects your unique interests and goals. When you do this you will no doubt find that you become much more motivated to learn and grow professionally. Furthermore, controlling your own professional development will result in more efficient use of your time—one of the scarcest commodities in a teacher's day. This is because your efforts will be focused on your specific needs, instead of those, say, a professional-development planner *thinks* are your needs.

Until now two major obstacles to successfully taking control of your professional development have existed: difficulty in accessing the necessary resources and trouble in finding colleagues with similar interests with whom to share ideas and discuss classroom experiences. Inevitably, teacher resource-centers and professional-development libraries are not conveniently located or their hours of operation don't suit your schedule. And when you do get there, the materials you want are either already taken out or they aren't available at that location. Without access to the materials you need when you need them, your efforts become stymied, often causing you to abandon a particular line of interest or inquiry. Also, colleagues at school never seem to have the time nor the inclination to sit down and discuss professional issues; and hurried faculty meetings or workshops always turn out to be the wrong forum to bring up substantive questions about teaching and learning. Research on teacher development has shown that one of the most effective ways for teachers to improve their classroom practice is to have the opportunity to reflect on and become articulate about what they've learned with colleagues, and then modify their approaches and discuss the changes. Without a collegial environment, individual initiative will be curtailed.

The Internet and Your Professional Development

Fortunately, a new tool, the Internet, can now help you take charge of your professional development. The obstacles of accessing resources and finding an interested professional community all but disappear with the Internet. Only a few years ago, the idea of using the Internet as a development tool would not have seemed plausible. Much has changed in the meantime, however. Not only is the Internet a vehicle for professional learning and growth, but arguably, it is the single most effective tool available today to help you improve professionally. Here are some of the reasons for this.

The Internet Is Readily Accessible

As recently as the early 1990s, the Internet was still mostly the exclusive domain of its originators—scientists, university researchers, and the military, who had access to it through their offices or laboratories, or through special dial-up arrangements from their homes. Teachers wanting access would have to approach one of those institutions, usually a university, and literally plead for permission to get connected. (I personally was the recipient of many such calls!) All of that changed almost overnight once word of the potential of the Internet got out from the stalwart pioneers who mastered the arcane commands and language then needed by computers. Schools, governments, corporations, and the public at large began to clamor for access. As a result, four major kinds of initiatives aimed at providing access began:

1. Federal and state education authorities, school districts, and individual schools simultaneously undertook plans to provide access to teachers and students. Most states now have operational plans in place with the goal of providing universal access to schools over the next few years. Estimates suggest that over half of the nation's schools now have some form of Internet access, and in a rapidly rising number of educational jurisdictions, all schools have access.

2. A new type of company, known as an Internet service provider (ISP), emerged to provide Internet connections to individual consumers and companies. Thousands of these companies now exist, specializing in either local or national coverage. These companies normally provide a full range of Internet services, a choice of usage and pricing options, customer help lines, and customized access software.

3. The major national online services, CompuServe, America Online, and Prodigy, until recently were networks unto themselves, allowing subscribers to communicate only with other subscribers of the same service and access only their service's resources. Now these services have lowered their rates and boast of how easily their subscribers can access the Internet.

4. Telephone and television cable companies jumped into the fray to offer either free or inexpensive access. They see commercial potential not in providing the access service itself, but rather in keeping customers loyal or in selling value-added news and entertainment services. AT&T began a service in 1996 to provide limited free access to the Internet to all its

long-distance customers. Most other telephone companies are pursuing similar kinds of plans for their customers. Cable companies, too, are either planning or providing Internet access that is higher speed than possible over ordinary telephone lines.

Now any teacher wanting Internet access has a variety of options from which to choose. Because of the commercial competition, access costs are decreasing rapidly too. By no means is the Internet universally accessible, but the signs are there that it is well on its way to being a mass communications medium accessible to all.

The Internet Is a Growing Medium

We have all heard media reports of how the Internet's growth rate is doubling every six months. What's even more remarkable is that this rate of growth continues unabated. One day soon growth will have to slow down, otherwise the number of Internet users will surpass the world's population! Still the Internet has room to grow: there are an estimated 660 million telephones in the world, yet only 7 million host computers are connected to the Internet. A sign of the popularity of the Internet is that the American public now spends at least as much time online as it does watching videos.

The Internet's growth is advantageous to professional development because with growth comes more people with interests similar to yours, greater diversity of ideas, increased resources, improvements in the technology, and a greater likelihood of finding exactly what you're looking for as more services become available. The downside of such rapid growth, however, is that communication line capacity sometimes cannot be expanded rapidly enough to meet the demand, resulting in delays and overloaded host computers.

The Internet Has a Friendly Face

The advent of the World Wide Web, together with the popularity of powerful home computers with graphics capabilities (e.g., Windows-based computers and Macintoshes), transformed the Internet from a hostile environment into a friendly, inviting world. Not so long ago the Internet was notorious for its arcane commands and jargon. While they still exist, you do not need to be very concerned about them, any more than you need to know much about how a car works to drive one. Once a computer is set up properly and Internet software is installed, a click of the mouse allows you to connect to the Internet, read text, see pictures, view movies, or hear music from anywhere in the world. Admittedly, the technology has glitches from time to time and busy signals are encountered more often than one would like. The Internet, nonetheless, has become easy enough to use so that you can focus on your professional-development goal at hand without the technology detracting you from your mission.

The Internet Has the Resources You Need

Futurists tell us that the amount of knowledge in the world doubles every eighteen months. A good part of that new knowledge now finds its way onto the Internet, in many cases even before it is published in the traditional media. Sometimes the information simply does not appear in the traditional media at all. (The Internet is credited with contributing to the downfall of the former Soviet Union because citizens were able to receive information directly rather than through a censored press.) Tens of millions of documents and resources are now available worldwide on the Internet, and thousands of projects and discussion groups of interest to teachers exist. A sampling:

- Reference works including databases of full-text articles, encyclopedias, maps, and original documents

- World Wide Web sites devoted specifically to teachers' needs, curriculum development, and professional activity

- Global collaborative projects involving teachers, students, and professionals from other disciplines

- Major newspapers, magazines, and professional journals

- Government reports, university resources, museums, archives, and libraries

- Discussion groups on every imaginable topic (and some you'd not wish to imagine!) and opportunities to chat online with leading international experts from the arts, industry, science, humanities, and the entertainment business

- Commercial consumer-oriented products and services, as well as low-cost or free software

Indeed, there are so many resources available that the Internet can easily become overwhelming. The challenge when you use the Internet for professional development—and for most other applications—is to locate quality resources that meet your needs. Generally speaking, there are no standards of quality on the Internet. Anybody can publish anything. A plethora of quality resources do exist, however, and in this book I'll point the way to some of these resources and give you strategies to find them yourself.

Beginning Assumptions

This book begins with the assumption that you have already had some, perhaps limited, experience using the Internet. For example, you may have occasionally browsed the World Wide Web, sent a few electronic-mail (e-mail) messages, and read about the Internet in magazines or professional journals. If you are not at this stage, many excellent books are available to help you. Please consult the appendix for some suggested readings that will serve as companions to this book.

Another assumption is that, from either school or home, you have a direct network connection to the Internet, or a dial-up connection via an ISP. Finally, the book assumes that you have either a Windows 3.1, Windows 95, or Macintosh computer and feel reasonably comfortable operating it.

Organization of the Book

The book is organized into five main sections:

1. The Internet and Its Essential Tools
2. Creating an Action Plan
3. Building Virtual Professional Communities
4. Doing Research on the Internet
5. Ahead to Tomorrow

The first four sections provide you with background information, practical advice, hints, and planning strategies to help you make the most of the Internet's potential. The last section deals with the future of the Internet and its implications for professional development. Here is a glimpse of what you'll find in each section and how this book can help you.

The Internet and Its Essential Tools

A day rarely goes by without news about the Internet appearing in the popular media. It has become a household word, but relatively few people know much about the Internet's nature. So a logical place to start is with a discussion of the Internet itself because, after all, this is the medium that will provide the opportunities for you to take charge of your professional development. I won't go into great detail about the Internet; however, you should have a basic framework for understanding how it operates. This framework will not only help you with reading this book, but it will serve you well for diagnosing problems when they occur (and they will!) and for understanding new technological advances.

After this discussion, I'll turn to two software tools that you will need to know how to use for almost all of your work on the Internet, e-mail software and a World Wide Web browser. For e-mail, I'll describe how to use the popular package Eudora Light. There's a good chance that you are already using Eudora. If not, you should still find the discussion helpful, as Eudora has many features common to other packages in use today and the hints and suggestions provided are applicable to any e-mail package. The Web browser that I'll describe is Netscape Navigator, the browser of choice by an estimated three-quarters of the market. Again, if you are not using Netscape, you'll find that the description of how to navigate, set bookmarks, and customize the software to suit your personal preferences will almost certainly apply to the browser you use.

Creating an Action Plan

In this section, you learn how to create your own professional-growth action plan. I recommend that you systematically plan your professional development, not just "let it happen." My contention is that the time you spend on the Internet will be more fruitful if you set yourself some goals and pursue them. I'm not advocating an overly rigid plan, rather one that has enough flexibility that you are able to explore areas of interest as they arise.

I begin the section with a discussion of how to set your own professional-development goals and to link them to the Internet. Following this, I discuss how to develop indicators so that you can tell when you've reached your goals. I conclude with suggestions on setting timelines to work toward your goals, keep track of where you've been on the Internet, what you've learned, and new directions you'd like to pursue.

Building Virtual Professional Communities

Once your action plan is in place and you understand the use of the key Internet tools, you are ready to begin exploiting the Internet for your own professional growth. Perhaps the most powerful characteristic of the Internet is its capability of enabling communication with others worldwide. We learn the most from communicating with others—sharing ideas, discussing controversial issues, asking questions, and testing hypotheses. This is the very essence of learning. When you join others regularly to communicate, you engage in what I refer to as community building. You build a "virtual community." A virtual community is defined by its members' sharing of common ideas, purpose, interests, or values. The difference between a "real" community and a virtual one is that members may be next door or a continent away!

You'll become familiar with the two main types of Internet virtual communities in this section: mailing lists and newsgroups. Mailing lists (also know as listservs) are essentially electronic-mail distribution lists. They are perhaps the easiest way for you to participate in a virtual community. You can simply join them, follow along by reading the discussion mailings, and participate when you feel confident and ready to contribute to the discussion. Internet newsgroups are the Internet's equivalent of community bulletin boards. They provide a forum for communities of interest to meet and discuss a whole range of ideas and issues. You will learn how newsgroups are structured, so that you can readily locate the ones you may wish to join, and how to participate in groups as a responsible Internet community member.

The section on community building will conclude with a look at other kinds of virtual professional communities: proprietary conferencing systems such as FirstClass, text-based chat systems, and live video conferencing. Although these communities don't have all the advantages of mailing lists and newsgroups, they do have worthy merits.

Doing Research on the Internet

In your professional-development plan, you will undoubtedly have a goal to find out more about a certain topic of interest. If you're an elementary teacher with students whose native tongue is not English, your goal may be to find out more about teaching English as a second language. If you're a high school teacher, you may wish to research the topic of "full inclusion" if your school district is considering adopting it as policy. You may also be enrolled in a graduate class and have a research assignment to undertake. Regardless of your specific research goal, this section of the book will help you reach it.

I'll begin the section with a discussion of why you would want to use the Internet in your research and what kind of information you can expect to find on it. Next, I'll describe the popular Web search tools available and show you how to use them. From there, I'll cover how to access and search bibliographic databases, including university and public libraries and the Educational Resources Information Collection (ERIC) system, a special database that you'll want to access over and over in your research. Although the Web is the most popular portion of the Internet, a discussion of search tools would not be complete without looking at tools to search other areas of the Internet. Therefore, I'll describe Archie for searching sites that have software, text, graphics, and other kinds of files available for downloading, Veronica for searching Gopher sites, and DejaNews for searching newsgroups. I'll end the section by helping you put all of what you've learned together and create a comprehensive search strategy.

Ahead to Tomorrow

Our discussion of how the Internet can help you grow professionally would not be complete without taking a glimpse into the future, to see both how the professional needs of teachers are evolving and where Internet technology is heading. Therefore, in the final section of this book I will focus on the directions these two forces are taking and how they are likely to intersect. In writing this section, however, my desire to make bold predictions about the future is tempered by a remark attributed to Will Rogers: "You can be on the right track—but still get run over!" This is especially true when you are talking about technology. So the section won't deal with trends that are a mere gleam in the eye of developers. I will talk, instead, about Internet technology that is already developed but not yet widely employed.

Part I

The Internet and Its Essential Tools

As teachers we are quick to realize that children have their own unique learning styles, and we adapt our teaching accordingly. But we are probably not as quick to acknowledge that adults, too, have their preferred ways of learning. When it comes to learning how to use computers, in particular, many of us freeze, not wanting to try anything new until the instructor shows us how to do it, for fear that we will break the computer or cause some terrible calamity. Others learn most effectively through trial and error. Here's an account from Angela Dawson, a teacher who recently completed her preservice program at York University's Faculty of Education and is beginning her teaching career, on how she learned to use the Internet and its tools. Angela makes the point that when learning has a purpose, it becomes much easier.

> My experiences in learning how to use the Internet have been equally exciting and frustrating. I have discovered that I learn to use technology best when I have a purpose in mind. For instance, in high school I programmed a computer to draw a house on the screen. Now I have no recollection as to *how* I drew the house, because the activity was meaningless to me. On the other hand, after beginning my teacher-education program, I had several opportunities to use technology as a tool for a real purpose.

My initial exposure to Internet technology was through Current Practice—the Faculty of Education's online conferencing system. I did not learn to use Current Practice by reading technical manuals or by learning the theory, but by becoming a conference moderator. In this role, I had to be online on a regular basis, guiding discussions via posting and responding to messages, and providing conference participants with information on educational resources from the Internet. Moderating made me use the technology quickly and, as a direct result, I became familiar enough with it so that I was able to get a job as a computer lab assistant.

Once I had begun exploring the educational resources on the Internet and saw how useful they would be to me as a future teacher, I felt that I wanted a set of Web pages that reflected my educational philosophies and interests and, at the same time, would provide other teachers with valuable resource links. So I set out to learn how to develop a Web site. When developing my site *(http://www.edu.yorku.ca/~tcs/~adawson/ angela.html),* my method once again did not involve reading manuals but began with hands-on exploration. To learn HyperText Markup Language (HTML), the language used for creating Web pages, I examined the HTML used in documents at other Web sites. I copied and pasted coding examples that I found were interesting and experimented with them. I followed the same approach when adding graphics to my pages. First I examined other graphics already drawn and experimented with them, one by one trying out the tools and filters in the graphics program I was using. Once I became familiar enough with the program, I scanned my own photographs and worked with them. I even began making my own graphics from scratch. While I enjoyed creating my own Web site, the most rewarding part came when I started receiving responses from teachers around the world who have found my pages useful for their own professional development.

In general, I must say that I prefer to learn by getting my hands on the technology, locking myself in a lab for a week to teach myself how to do it. Someone showing me will not help me learn, and someone standing over my shoulder will cause me to use the technology less competently than I would if they just let me be. I continue to learn more each time I explore the Internet and its tools.

Below is the story of how another teacher, Stella Sanchez, learned to use the Internet. Stella is a bilingual teacher at Marilyn Burns Elementary in Brownsville, Texas. She also prefers hands-on learning but cautions us that, when exploring online, we need to keep focused on our task.

I have been teaching for eight years at Burns, a large multitrack school with some fifteen hundred students from pre-K through fifth grade. While I am a fairly experienced computer user, I consider myself somewhat of an advanced novice when it comes to the

Internet. Right now, I am using the Internet to conduct research on how technology is useful in the classroom, for a master's program in educational technology in which I'm enrolled. I also use it to gain information for my daily lesson plans on topics of interest to my students, and from time to time I download games or educational software for my classroom. I work with year-round themes in social studies and science and math and how they integrate with the reading and comprehension. The Internet offers countless sources of information for these projects too. Unfortunately, my school is not yet connected to the Net, so the best I can do for the children in my class at present is to bring in resources, such as graphs, charts, and reports, that I get from the Internet at home for their use.

Although I was first introduced to the Web in my graduate program, I feel I learn it best by experimenting on my own, doing such things as entering words into search engines and seeing what results I get. Admittedly, it does help to take a training session from someone who can offer tips and shortcuts on how to locate information, to avoid running into countless links that really don't benefit your purposes. I know some school districts have already set up some Internet training sessions to do just that, as they know teachers just don't have the time to learn these tricks on their own.

I would say that one of the hardest things for me in learning to use the Internet was to get out of the habit of following every link that I came across. I tended to get carried away following all the interesting links, so that I often forgot what it was I had begun searching for! I often got lost and had to find my way back and force myself to become more focused on my immediate task. Once I became more familiar with the Internet and got into the habit of keeping focused, this became less and less a problem.

Another difficulty was that I could not really locate the information I wanted because there was just so much available. It often became frustrating. So I learned to use keywords and connecting words and concentrated on those words only, without getting off track.

My best recommendation to others wanting to learn the Internet for their professional development is to focus and not get carried away with surfing the Net. The Internet is a tremendous resource, so it's well worth your time to make an effort to use it properly.

1 | What Do I Need to Know About the Internet?

In the introduction, I said that you don't need to know much about the Internet itself to be able to use it effectively for your professional development. I likened navigating the Internet to driving a car, in that you don't need to know much about the inner workings of a car to drive one. That's true, but just as you need to know some basics about a car such as when to have the oil changed and where the spare tire can be found, you need to know some fundamentals about the Internet, so that you're not navigating blindly. The concepts you should be familiar with include:

- The nature of the Internet
- Internet clients and servers
- Internet software tools
- Internet addresses
- The language of the Internet

I will not go into any more detail about these concepts than what's necessary for you to develop a basic framework for understanding how the Internet functions. This framework will be necessary in order for you to follow the discussions in this book. Moreover, it should put you in good stead in dealing with the inevitable problems that you'll encounter on your journeys across the Internet.

The Nature of the Internet

Information superhighway, infobahn, global village, and cyberspace are just some of the names people use when they talk about the Internet. After hearing all of the hype about the Internet, you may be left wondering what it really is. The answer depends upon what level of detail you want—and even when you ask the question—because it's a constantly evolving entity!

Sufficient for us is the definition that the Internet is a worldwide network of computer networks. Imagine, for a moment, if your school had a computer network and it was linked to a nearby school's network. You would then have a network of two networks. Similarly, if that other school's network was linked to a local university's network, you would then have a network of three networks. Now picture that university's network being linked to all other university networks in the state, which in turn were linked to other university, government, and commercial networks in the country. You can see that if this pattern were extended farther afield, we'd soon have a worldwide network of networks. Well, that's exactly what the Internet is and how it came into being. No one said "Now let's have a worldwide computer network" and sat down and wrote a master plan. It simply evolved by networks joining together one by one.

The Internet's roots are in the late 1960s, with ARPAnet, a U.S. Defense Department research network. The Defense Department designed the basic technology that allowed researchers, using far-flung computers of different manufacturers, to communicate with each other over unreliable communications circuits. In the late 1980s, the National Science Foundation (NSF) wanted to link five major university supercomputer centers that they had created. They tried to use ARPAnet, but the effort was unsuccessful. So they built their own network, NSFnet, using ARPAnet's technology. This effort was extremely successful and, because of the NSF's policy of promoting universal educational access to the network, more and more educational institutions in North America and abroad, governments, and research organizations started linking to NSFnet. By the early 1990s, schools, libraries, and businesses worldwide began connecting to the network in droves, and the Internet as a worldwide network of networks came into being.

Originally, the philosophy of the Internet was very much based on the motto of computer hackers of the 1970s and 1980s: Information Shall Be Free. That's why you'll find a tremendous amount of sharing and exchanging of information, even software, on the Internet. Any commercial activity was sternly rebuked by the Internet community, often by "flaming" the offender (i.e., hurtling verbal abuse via e-mail or newsgroup postings). Cultures are never stagnant, though, and with the rapid influx of commercial Internet connections in the mid-1990s, the commercialization of the Net began. Today the promotion and sale of goods and services on the Web is commonplace. Some Internet sites charge for access to their services. However, unsolicited advertising via e-mail and newsgroup posting is still frowned upon by the Internet community and anyone who violates this unwritten rule does so at their peril.

Interestingly, there is no single authority that controls the Internet. Each member network sets its own policies and procedures for use. Ed Kroll, author of the popular text *The Whole Internet: User's Guide and Catalog* (1992; 2d ed. 1994), describes the Internet as being governed much like a church. There is a council of elders that decides how the congregation should behave, but as a member of the congregation you can either accept or reject what the council says. The council, in the case of the Internet, is the Internet Society, a voluntary organization whose purpose is to promote global information exchange. Like a church, the society asks members for their opinions on various technical matters and creates standards based on those opinions. If members want to communicate fully with other Internet member networks, then they adopt the standards. If they don't, that's fine, too, provided they don't do anything that harms the Internet. The same happens in a church: you can usually remain a member as long as you don't radically depart from its teachings.

Often it is said that the Internet is free. Someone connecting to it from their school or university may in fact think so. This is far from the truth, however. Even if you personally don't pay for online service, somebody does. Probably it's your school district or university. There is no central fee-collecting authority for the Internet. Each member network pays for the connection from its own network to another member network, the other member network pays for the connection to still another member network, and so on. You pay a service provider to gain Internet access so that your provider can pay for a connection to another member.

Internet Clients and Servers

When computers are connected to the Internet they perform one of two functions: they operate as *clients* or *servers*. Servers are typically powerful computers with high-capacity hard disks. These computers store the data that you want to access, whether they are World Wide Web pages, library databases, picture files, software for downloading, or Internet newsgroups. Servers are usually left running continuously, waiting to be contacted by other computers with instructions to perform certain tasks. The computers that initiate these instructions are called clients. Your personal computer at home or school plays this client role.

In order for clients and servers to "talk" to each other, they need to have a common language. That language is called a protocol, which is essentially a set of rules governing how computers communicate. Two protocols are necessary for clients and servers to communicate over the Internet. The first protocol, called Transmission Control Protocol/Internet Protocol (TCP/IP), sees that messages sent over the Internet arrive, intact, where they should. All computers connected to the Internet have software that supports the TCP/IP protocol. The second protocol, called the application protocol, is associated with the software program that allows clients and servers to accomplish various tasks. For instance, if you want to log on to a remote server, both your client and the server must have software that supports the Telnet protocol. Or if you want to browse the World Wide Web, both client and server must have software that supports the HyperText Transfer Protocol (HTTP).

Once clients and servers have the required software to understand each other, they are ready to interact. I'll illustrate their interaction using HTTP, the protocol that you will likely use the most often. Not all Internet protocols function exactly the same as HTTP, the Web protocol, however the principle is the same for all.

Suppose you are browsing the Web home page for York University, the institution where I work. On the page you'll notice underlined text. This kind of text is called a *hypertext link*, because when you click your mouse on it you are taken to another Web page. Pictures and graphics may also function as links. For this illustration, let's say you click on the link *About York University*. This is what happens:

1. York's Web server—like all servers—patiently waits to receive instructions from Web clients. Your Web client acts on your instruction to link to About York University and confirms an address for this link.

2. Using the address associated with the link and HTTP, the client contacts the Web server at York University and tells it to send the document About York University.

3. The server responds by sending the document to the client along with any other media, such as pictures or sound associated with the document. (The document it sends back contains HyperText Markup Language (HTML) "tags" that tell the client how to display the document on your computer screen.)

4. The client displays the document on your computer screen, closes the connection with York University, lets the server take a rest, and takes a break itself, waiting until you click on something else or type in an address.

Note that you do not make an actual connection to the Web server—you just send it a message and it sends you back a reply. While the Web server is getting information for you, it may also be handling requests from many other clients around the world. If it's a popular server, you should not be surprised if you get delays in receiving a response to your request, or even the occasional message saying "connection refused" because the server was busy. Servers may also refuse a connection because they are "down" for maintenance.

Internet Protocols and Software Tools

The application protocols I just mentioned, Telnet and HTTP, are just two out of seven protocols that you'll encounter when using the Internet. For each of these protocols, there's client software readily available for Macintosh and Windows computers. Often these software tools are supplied to you by your school, university, or Internet service provider when you get your Internet connection. All are available, via the Internet, at no cost to educators. You should think of these software tools as seven *categories* of tools, really, as there are often many different versions of the same tool, just as there are many different versions of word processors. Following is a brief description of each of these protocols and their tools.

HyperText Transfer Protocol

As you saw previously, the Web uses the HyperText Transfer Protocol, or HTTP. Developed in 1990 at CERN, Geneva's European Laboratory for Particle Physics, as a way for scientists to share research in the high-energy-physics community, the Web is now the most common way to access information on the Internet. So popular has the Web become that many people use the term "Web" and "Internet" interchangeably, although the Web is just one of many different ways to exchange data on the Internet.

The Web is based on what's known as *hypertext* system. If you've ever used the Help system in Microsoft Windows or Macintosh's System Guide, you're well on your way toward understanding what hypertext is. Here is how it works: When you click with your mouse on an underlined word or words on a page in a hypertext system, you immediately link to another page of the document or to an entirely different document. A major difference between your computer's Help system and the Web is that clicking on words on a Web page may link you to a document on a computer on the other side of the world, instead of to another page or document on your computer. And then when you click on a word in that document, you may be taken to a computer somewhere else in the world. If you imagine tens of millions of documents spread over hundreds of thousands of computers that are connected to the Internet throughout the world, with many documents having links to others, you can see how the "World Wide Web" got its name. Literally, the Web is a global intertwined network of information.

The Web has evolved into much more than merely a hypertext system of text documents, however. Web pages are now frequently enriched with graphics, pictures, audio, animation, and video, so the Web could more accurately be described as a *hypermedia* system. The software you use to view Web pages is called a *Web browser*. In this book, I'll focus on the use of Netscape Navigator, the most widely used browser for Windows and Macintosh, because it can also accomplish many of the same tasks as other Internet tools.

Gopher

Gopher, developed at the University of Minnesota, is a menu-based system for accessing information. When you connect to a Gopher site on the Internet, you are typically presented with a menu, much like the table of contents of a book. You then click on the heading that likely contains what you're interested in, and navigate your way through successive layers of submenus until you find the item you want.

Gopher was very popular before the Web surpassed it in the mid-1990s. Few new Gopher sites are being constructed, but many of the remaining sites still have valuable resources. Netscape can be used to access Gopher sites.

Telnet

With Telnet you are actually able to log on to a remote computer on the Internet and operate just as though you were connected to it directly. The most common use of Telnet now is to access remote databases, such as library catalogs. You'll need a password and ID for the remote computer if it's a private machine; however, many computers on the Internet have public services that can be accessed without an ID or by using one that's publicly known (e.g., "guest").

You'll encounter two different "flavors" of Telnet: one uses a protocol known as VT100, which allows you to connect to UNIX computers; the other is TN3270, which connects you to IBM mainframe computers. VT100 and TN3270 client software can be linked to Netscape to allow it to make Telnet connections. I'll talk more about this in Chapter 3.

FTP

While Telnet allows you to log on to a remote computer, one thing you cannot do with Telnet is retrieve files from that computer. The File Transfer Protocol (FTP) was developed for this purpose. Files you might want to retrieve from a remote computer may be text, pictures, or even software. Again, you'll need a password and ID to use FTP if the remote computer is private. Many computers, however, are set up for public retrieval of files. The convention that's used for public access is to log on with the ID of "anonymous" and enter your e-mail address when prompted for a password. Netscape can be used for FTP, although some experienced Internet users prefer separate FTP client software such as Fetch or Rapid Filer.

Internet News

The Internet has well over twenty thousand newsgroups that can be accessed. Known as Usenet newsgroups, they are the Internet's equivalent of electronic bulletin boards, where individuals "post" messages to be seen and responded to by interested readers. Newsgroups use the Network News Transfer Protocol (NNTP). I'll be talking more about how newsgroups can be used for professional development later in this book in the section on virtual professional communities. Newsgroups can be accessed with Netscape, but again, many experienced users prefer to use separate client software. Newswatcher is a popular news client.

Internet Mail

You may not have a choice in the e-mail software you use because your school, university, or Internet service provider will provide you with a mail client compatible with your institution's mail server. Whichever mail package you use, you should realize that when you send mail to someone, it goes out over the Internet in a form known as Simple Mail Transfer Protocol (SMTP). Because of SMTP, someone using Microsoft Mail on the Macintosh, for example, can send a message to someone using UNIX mail and can count on it arriving in a readable form. Netscape can be used for e-mail, although I will describe later how to use the more popular e-mail tool Eudora.

Internet Relay Chat

If you want to have an electronic conversation with someone else on the Internet (not with voice, but with text), you'll be using software that supports yet another protocol known as Internet Relay Chat (IRC). You can use a separate chat client, but I recommend that you use Netscape together with chat "helper" software for simplicity. Netscape helpers will be discussed in Chapter 3 and the application of chat to professional development in the section on virtual communities.

Internet Addresses

All computers on the Internet have a unique address, just as all houses have addresses so that they can be distinguished from other houses. Houses may contain many different people, so when you address a letter, you not only put the home address but the name of the intended recipient on the envelope. You have to do the same on the Internet: if you want to access a particular resource on the Internet, you have to give the name of the resource, the address of the computer, and where the resource is located on that computer. On the other hand, if you're sending electronic mail, you need the intended receiver's e-mail name and the address of the computer through which the person receives mail.

Addresses for Internet resources are called URLs, short for Uniform Resource Locators. There are three parts to a URL: the protocol, the host name, and the directory. Here's a typical URL.

http://www.heyu.edu/faculty/home.html

From this URL, you are able to discern the following information:

• The URL is for a Web connection, designated by the protocol *http*. The protocol is the part of the URL to the left of the double forward slashes (//). Other protocols that you might see in a URL are: FTP for an FTP connection; Gopher for a Gopher connection; News for a Newsgroup connection; and Telnet for a Telnet connection.

• The URL directs you to a computer named *www.heyu.edu*. This part of the URL is called the host name. No two computers can have the same host name, just like no two households could have the same telephone number. The host name consists of two parts, *www*, the name given to a specific computer in an organization, and *heyu.edu*, which is called the domain name. The left part of the domain name, *heyu*, is the name of the organization; the right part, *edu*, is called the top-level domain. In the United States, the top-level domain indicates the nature of the organization: *edu* for education; *gov* for government; *com* for commercial; *net* for computer networks; and *org* for other kinds of organizations. No other countries make this distinction; instead they simply have a two-letter country code for the top-level domain (e.g., AU for Australia; CA for Canada; and JP for Japan). Occasionally you'll see Internet addresses listed simply as four groups of numbers separated by periods (e.g., 128.54.123.12). This is a perfectly valid address form. Every Internet address starts off as a number but, because numbers are hard to remember, names are usually associated with the numbers too. However, from time to time you'll encounter a numeric address because the owner of the computer simply did not register a name for it.

• The document, named *home.html*, is located in a directory called *faculty*. If you're familiar with Windows computers, you'll recognize */faculty/home.html* as the "path" for the file *home.html*. If you're a Macintosh user, think of directories as folders. Sometimes in a path, the file name is omitted because the file being referenced will be accessed by default. When you're entering URLs, you normally don't have to worry about whether to use upper- or lowercase letters. There are some exceptions, so it's always wise to note addresses exactly as they're written. URLs *never* contain blank spaces. Words are joined by an underscore (_) as in *http://www.heyu.edu/book_club*.

E-mail addresses follow the same basic format as URLs, except that in front of the host name you put the person's e-mail name followed by the "@" sign. For example,

jdoe@mail.heyu.edu

sends mail to the user *jdoe* at the computer *mail.heyu.edu.*

When people first started using e-mail, addresses were difficult to recognize and remember because people frequently used impersonal numbers such as CS98765 for their user name. Now most people use various combinations of their names and initials so they are easy to recognize. E-mail addresses are *never* case sensitive, nor do they ever have blanks.

Learning the Language of the Internet

After reading this chapter your head may be spinning with the specialized language of the Internet. No doubt you are asking yourself, "How much of this do I *really* have to know?" Ideally, you should at least understand the general concepts covered. You can always refer back to this chapter as needed. I've distilled key concepts into the following three main points:

1. Protocols are the common language that computer clients and servers follow when they talk to each other.

2. All Internet resources have addresses, called URLs, which begin with a protocol name and are followed by the computer host name and directory. E-mail addresses are similar, but begin with a person's name followed by the @ sign and the host name. Neither have blank spaces in them.

3. HTTP is a protocol you'll use frequently because it is the prefix to every Web address. FTP, Telnet, Gopher, IRC, Newsgroups, and Internet Mail are protocols too, but more important is to know that they are the generic names of different software tools that let you accomplish certain tasks over the Internet.

2

Making the Most
of Your Electronic Mail

One of the essential sets of skills you will need in order to take control of your professional development with the Internet is electronic mail capability. This is because e-mail provides a vital link to teachers and others around the world with whom you can share ideas, discuss practice, seek help, offer and receive advice, and learn of new developments. E-mail can free you from having limited access to peers, providing a world of colleagues to draw on.

You should realize, however, that being an effective user of e-mail goes beyond knowing the "mechanics" of how to send and receive mail. Whenever a new form of communication arises, cultural norms evolve surrounding its proper use. Consider the telephone. Conversations begin with an exchange of greetings wherein the caller is identified, followed by the actual conversation, which may be very brief—to the point where if it took place face-to-face it would be considered rude—and then ends with a salutation. So too are there norms surrounding what is deemed by the Internet community as acceptable use of e-mail and, more so, unacceptable use. Accordingly, throughout this discussion on how to make the most of your e-mail, I will weave in hints and suggestions about the conventions of acceptable e-mail use.

Although I'm assuming that you have used e-mail to some extent already, you probably are not familiar with all of the features of your e-mail software package. Therefore, in this chapter I will focus on moving beyond the simple sending and receiving of messages, by describing how to make use of the various sending features likely to be found in your software. Then I will discuss how to manage your e-mail messages, so that once you actively use e-mail and subscribe to mailing lists you are not overwhelmed by the sheer volume of your mail.

Throughout this chapter, I will illustrate my discussion using the e-mail software package Eudora Light. There is a good chance that you use this popular package for Macintosh and Windows, as it is commonly found in schools and universities. This chapter will still be of value to you if you use a different package, because the features of your software will almost certainly be similar; also, I will only mention features that are likely to be found in all of the newer graphics e-mail software packages.

Eudora Light and Mail Systems

Eudora Light is an easy-to-use e-mail client software package that is available for free from many Internet FTP sites, as well as from Qualcomm Inc., its commercial distributor. Qualcomm not only supports Eudora Light, but sells a more full-featured version of the software called Eudora Pro. For the sake of brevity, I will refer to Eudora Light as simply Eudora. (If you're wondering how an e-mail software package got such a strange name, it's because Steve Dorner, the developer, named the software after the writer Eudora Welty, author of a story entitled "Why I Live at the P.O.")

There are two general methods of accessing e-mail using clients on personal computers: *offline* and *online*. In the offline method, clients and servers communicate using a standard Internet protocol known as POP (Post Office Protocol). Eudora uses the offline method, therefore it is often referred to as a POP mail client. When you send or receive mail with Eudora and other POP clients, the client connects briefly to your host mail server—just long enough to transfer mail between the server and your computer, then the connection is terminated. POP mail systems are popular because owners of mail servers don't have to maintain large amounts of hard-disk space to store all of the mail messages of their users. The mail servers only have to store unaccessed mail; the users' local computer stores the mail once it's transferred from the server. This can be a problem, however, if you frequently check your mail from more than one location, such as from home, from school, or when you travel, because in order to read your mail it has to be transferred to a local computer. As a result, you may have your mail scattered over several different computers, making it inconvenient if you want to reread messages you've already looked at from a different machine. Some POP servers support a feature that permits you to leave your mail on the server; however, this feature has a reputation for being unreliable, so check with the operator of your mail system before using it.

The online e-mail method requires that you remain logged on to your mail server while you deal with your messages. Your mail is normally stored on the server, so that no matter where you read your mail from, you always have access to it. There is an Internet standard protocol for online mail, Internet Message Access Protocol (IMAP), that is starting to become popular, but it is not yet in widespread use. Most online mail systems use protocols developed and owned by the vendor of the system. FirstClass, a popular e-mail and computer conferencing system in schools, is one of them. Online mail systems sometimes have clients that allow you to work offline with your mail.

About the only difference in general operation that you will notice between online and offline systems—albeit an extremely important one—is how the two systems handle the storage of messages. On a practical level, if you have to pay for your Internet connection time, online systems can be more expensive to use than POP systems because, unless your system has an offline client, you need to be connected while you read and compose your messages.

Sending Messages

The window for sending a new message in your e-mail software will likely have four distinct parts: a title bar along the top of the message, a bar showing a row of icons, the message-header information area, and the message-body area. Eudora's new-message screen is shown in Figure 2–1.

Figure 2–1

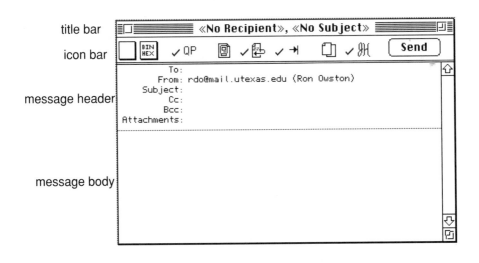

Title Bar

When you first open the window to send a message, you'll note that the title bar reads *<<No Recipient>>*, *<<No Subject>>*. This information will remain that way until you either send your message or queue it for sending later. Once you take either of these actions, the recipient information will automatically be obtained from the *To:* and *Subject:* lines in the message header. This information will be useful to you when you decide to either file for future reference or delete the copy of the message that you've just sent.

Icon Bar

Beneath the title bar is the icon bar. The rightmost icon is the *Send* button, which is self-explanatory. Immediately to the left of this is the *Signature* icon. When this icon is checked, your signature is automatically added to the bottom of your e-mail message, although you won't see it on your screen when you're composing your message. To create your signature, select *Signature* from the *Window* main pull-down menu bar across the top of your screen. You will then see a blank window into which you can enter your name and other relevant personal information.

A generally accepted guideline is not to exceed four to six lines for your signature. The minimum information you should include is your name and Internet address. Many people neglect to include their Internet address, but it should be provided as a courtesy to others. Because of the various Internet routing information that mail servers add to messages, it's sometimes difficult for receivers of mail to determine the originator's address. By adding this information, you provide recipients with your correct address for future reference. In addition to the minimum information, some Internet users like to add their title and affiliation as well as telephone and fax numbers. Others like to add a witty quotation or saying as part of their signature or even cute line drawings. I don't advise this, as recipients may see such superfluous matter as an annoyance after they get several messages from you.

To the left of the Signature icon, you will see an icon illustrating two sheets of paper; this is the *Keep Copy* icon. When this icon is checked, a copy of the message that you are sending is kept in the out mailbox. If you are unsure of whether to check this icon, you should probably err on the safe side by checking it. You can always delete copies of any messages you don't want at a later date. But be diligent about deleting unwanted copies, because if you use e-mail a lot, the out mailbox can quickly grow and consume unnecessary hard-disk space.

The remaining icons represent advanced features that determine the format of your message and any attachments. I won't discuss these features here; you can consult the

Eudora manual if you want to find out more about them. For now leave them checked and set the way they appear in the illustration.

Message Header

Below the icon bar is the message-header area. As you can see, it contains headings identical to those of a typical printed office memo. The *To:* field is the area into which you enter the recipient's Internet e-mail address. If you want to send the message to more than one person, there's no need to address and send it separately to each one. You can simply enter all of the recipients' addresses at once, provided that you separate each by a comma. (Note that other mail programs may require you to enter each recipient's address on a separate line.) Since it is an effortless process to send mail to many people at once, newcomers to e-mail tend to add names to the list of recipients "just in case" they may be interested. Always think twice before you add extra names, however. Ask yourself if the message will indeed be of interest to prospective recipients. If you are not judicious in addressing your mail, you may find others deleting your messages without reading them, because as soon as they see your name, they'll just assume it's more "junk mail" from you!

Whenever you create a new message, Eudora automatically inserts your e-mail address and name in the *From:* field. When your software was installed, you or the person who installed it for you would have entered this information into Eudora. If you wanted to change any of this information you would select *Settings* from the *Special* main pull-down menu bar and make the changes in the appropriate boxes.

The *Subject:* field is immediately below the *From:* field. While its purpose is self-explanatory, many people new to the Internet leave this field blank. If you do this, you've committed a breach in what the Internet community considers to be proper use of e-mail. Recipients expect to see a subject indicated, to provide a context for the message they've just received. Furthermore, the subject field gives them an indication of which messages they should read first if they have many unread messages to deal with. Therefore, I recommend that you always fill this field in, using no more than several keywords that accurately describe the topic of your message.

The next two fields, *Cc:* and *Bcc:* are labels that are holdovers from the days when photocopiers were not found in offices and carbon paper was used to make copies of handwritten or typewritten letters and memos. The fields denote carbon copy and blind carbon copy, respectively. If you want a copy of your e-mail message to go to someone, usually for information purposes, you list their e-mail address in the *Cc:* field. The main recipient of the message can then see who received a duplicate of the message. If you enter an e-mail address in the *Bcc:* field, that person receives a copy of the message without the main recipient knowing you sent him or her a copy. Some people never use the *Bcc:* field because they feel that it's not ethical to send someone a copy of a message without the main recipient knowing. Whether or not you use this field is your decision. My only caution when you send copies of messages to others is that you do so after deliberation, for the same reasons I mentioned above.

Nicknames

As you begin to use e-mail more and more, you'll find that there are some people you send messages to very often. There is a feature found in Eudora—and most other mail packages—that eliminates the necessity of entering a full e-mail address each time you send someone a message. This is the nicknames feature. For example, if you often send a message to a colleague named Ed Jones who has the e-mail address *ejones@tiger.heyu.edu,* you can create a nickname for him—for example, "Ed"—so that you only have to enter this shortened version in the *To:, Cc:,* or *Bcc:* fields. Eudora will then automatically provide the complete address.

To create a nickname with Eudora, select *Nicknames* from the *Window* pull-down menu. When you do this you will see the Nicknames dialogue box. You begin by clicking on *New* and entering the person's nickname, full e-mail address, and any reference notes about the person, as illustrated in Figure 2–2.

Figure 2–2

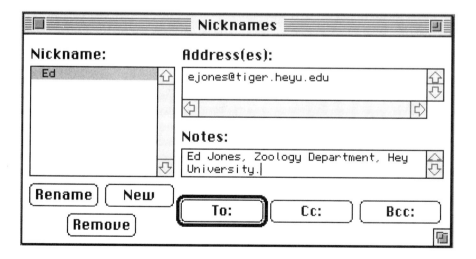

You can then save the nickname for future reference by clicking on the square in upper-left corner and closing the window. If you are in the process of composing a new message, clicking on *To:*, *Cc:*, or *Bcc:* before closing inserts the nickname into the appropriate field in the header of the new message.

You can also use the nicknames feature to conveniently create a group mailing list. Say you frequently send mail to all colleagues in your department and wanted to avoid entering their full addresses each time. You simply give your group a nickname (e.g., Department), and in the *Address(es)* box you enter the addresses of all the members you want to include, either one per line followed by a return or separated by commas. Note that if you already have a nickname for any of the relevant members, you need only to enter that in order for their full address to be recorded.

Attachments

When you're corresponding with colleagues, you may wish to send them documents that you've created on your word processor (or possibly even software, provided, of course, you are not prohibited by copyright from doing this). These items can be sent as attachments to your e-mail message. Attachments are analogous to enclosures you put in an envelope in the regular mail. They accompany the e-mail message as "riders" and do not appear in the main body of your message. Some of the reasons you might send documents as attachments rather than including them in the body of the message would be: (1) you are collaborating with a colleague on writing an article and for convenience want to keep the document in the format of the word processor you are both using, (2) you want to keep the formatting of an original document so that items like indentations, columns, highlights, and fonts—which are lost in an e-mail message—are maintained, or (3) the item you want to send is too long to include in the main body of an e-mail message (some e-mail systems restrict the length of messages).

To attach a document to a Eudora message, you select *Attach Document* from the *Message* pull-down menu. You will then see a dialogue box. Locate and highlight the document you want to attach, and then click on *Open*. The name of the document will then appear in the *Attachments* field. Note that Eudora will not allow you to type the name of the document into the field directly. If you change your mind about the attachment, you can click anywhere on the document name in the Attachments field and delete it. You can also repeat the procedure if you wish to attach more than one document.

When you send an attachment to others, you should realize that the recipients may not be able to read it if they use a different word processor or different computer operating system. For example, there's no guarantee that if you send a Macintosh Word 6.0 document to a person with WordPerfect for Windows they will be able to read it, unless they have special conversion software. So it's always a good idea to check with recipients in advance to make sure their system is compatible with the format of the document you're attaching.

Message Body

Again, it is self-evident that you type your message in the large blank area called the message-body field. Since the editing features are rather limited in most e-mail programs and many don't have a spell checker, you may wish to compose your message with your favorite word processor first. When you're happy with what you've written, you can then highlight (with the mouse) the text of your message in your word processor, copy it by selecting *Copy* from the *Edit* pull-down menu, and paste it into the message body area of Eudora by choosing *Paste* from Eudora's *Edit* pull-down menu.

However you wish to compose your message, there are several points to bear in mind: First, make sure to type continuously and not hit the *Return* key at the end of each line, because the text will wrap around automatically. Second, as mentioned previously, don't bother to apply any special formatting or fonts to the body of your text. They will simply be stripped out of your message when it is sent over the Internet, or worse, appear as a string of indecipherable control characters. If you want to add emphasis to a word or phrase, there are some Internet conventions for doing so:

• for a mild emphasis, add asterisks before and after the part you want to highlight (e.g., "this is the *most* important principle");

• for a stronger emphasis, put the word or phrase in upper-case letters (e.g., "I will meet you on THURSDAY, not Friday"). But never type the entire text of your message in upper case, BECAUSE THIS IS THE INTERNET'S EQUIVALENT OF SHOUTING AT SOMEONE.

A third point is to keep your messages reasonably terse and to the point. Text can be difficult to read on the screen. Furthermore, the recipient may have to be online while reading your message and pay for connection time. A rough guideline is to keep your messages to about one screen in length. If your message needs to be longer, you probably should write it in your word processor and attach the file to the message as I explained above.

Finally, with regard to the actual content of your message, never include anything that is strictly confidential. E-mail can be easily forwarded to anyone, anywhere, by the recipient, either accidentally or on purpose. Your message might also be legitimately read by computer-system administrators if the message cannot be delivered or if it is causing problems to the system. Some experienced users advise you to never say anything that you would not mind seeing on the evening news! Moreover, always read through your messages several times before sending them. Remember that the recipient has no non-verbal clues about what you are saying. For example, if you wrote "John is a real winner," the recipient may interpret that statement literally, as meaning that John is successful, or ironically, as meaning that John is, in fact, a loser. You should also ask yourself, "Would I send this message tomorrow morning?" This is particularly important when you are responding to an emotional issue, because once a message is sent it cannot be retrieved.

Sending Versus Queuing Messages

When you finish composing your message, you have two options for sending it. You can click on the *Send* button and the message will be sent immediately, provided you are already connected to the Internet. Or if you are composing several messages, you can queue them so that they are sent in a batch when you finish composing all of them. The queuing feature is convenient and possibly a cost-saver if you have to pay an hourly rate for your Internet connection. To enable the queuing feature, select the *Settings* item under the *Special* pull-down menu. Click on the *Sending Mail* icon at the left of the screen and then make sure that there is no X in the top box beside the heading *Immedi-ate send*.

After you do this you will notice that the *Send* button for new messages has changed to *Queue*. Clicking on the *Queue* button will hold your message in the outgo-ing mailbox. When you are ready to send all of your queued messages, click on *Send Queued Messages* under the *File* pull-down menu.

Receiving Messages

Three steps are necessary to read your messages with a POP mail client such as Eudora. First you need to connect to the Internet. This is not necessary if your computer is always connected to the Internet at your school or office; however, if you access the Internet by modem, you must first dial up your Internet service provider to make the connection.

Second, you must tell your mail server to download new messages to your computer. This is done in Eudora by selecting *Check Mail* from the *File* menu. When you do this, you will see a message telling you either that you have or do not have new mail. Any new mail that you have is placed in your In mailbox and it remains there indefinitely unless you decide to delete it or move it to another mailbox.

Third, you must open your In mailbox by going to the *Mailbox* pull-down menu and selecting *In*. The In mailbox is illustrated in Figure 2–3. You can see that the message summaries are arranged chronologically, with the most recent message at the top. In the

Figure 2–3

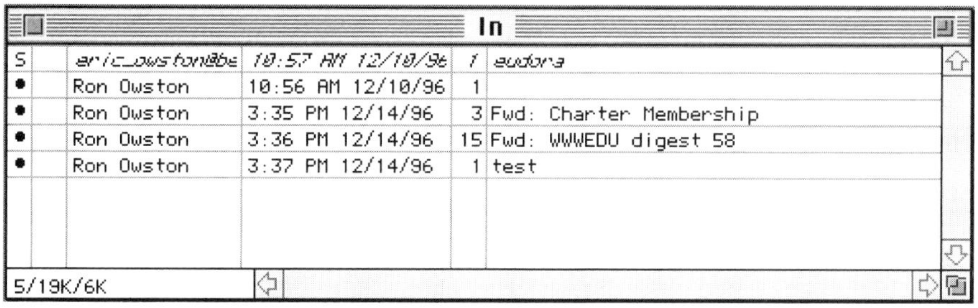

leftmost column of the mailbox a dot appears beside any unread messages. To the right of this you see the name of the message sender, the time and date the message was sent, the size of the message in kilobytes (k), and the subject of the message. To view a message, double click anywhere on the message summary line.

Note that three numbers appear in the bottom left corner of the mailbox. These numbers indicate from left to right the number of messages in your mailbox (5), the space those messages require in kilobytes (19k), and the amount of wasted hard-disk space in the mailbox (6k). Eudora will occasionally recover this wasted space on its own; however, it's a good idea to keep an eye on the wasted space, because it can be used for other purposes. If you are short of space on your hard drive, simply go to the *Special* pull-down menu and choose *Compact Mailboxes* to eliminate all wasted space.

Replying to Messages

When you select *Reply* from the *Message* pull-down menu, Eudora will display the sender's message as highlighted text, with ">" marks appearing to the left of each line. The ">" marks are the standard Internet way of quoting. If you do not wish to quote any of the sender's message, press the *Delete* key. The sender's message will be erased and then you can enter your reply. Frequently, though, when replying to messages, you want to answer questions posed by the sender or comment on certain parts of the message. Below is an illustration of how this feature can be a great convenience by avoiding the need to retype the sender's message. Note that my responses do not have the ">" sign beside them.

>I would like to know if you will be attending the
>faculty meeting tomorrow.

No, I won't, because I have a dentist appointment at 3:30.
>and if you won't be, what is your opinion about the
>motion to cancel classes for the field trip.
I'm opposed! We've canceled too many classes so far this year. I'm having trouble keeping up with the syllabus.

When you are finished with your reply, you have the choice of either sending it immediately or queuing it to be sent later, following exactly the same method I described above for sending a new message.

The Sendability Test

Throughout this chapter I've pointed out what is considered proper Internet e-mail usage. Clearly, like dinner table manners or social etiquette, these suggestions are not based on hard and fast rules but on what most people agree is the proper way to behave. You may choose not to follow them and never hear a negative word. I know I've pondered whether to mention minor breaches of conduct to colleagues who are novice e-mail users for fear that I will hurt their feelings. On the other hand, you may find yourself chastised by recipients of your messages. To prevent this from happening, I'll offer one overriding question to ask yourself before clicking the *Send* button: Would you like to receive the message you're about to send? Try to look at your message objectively to see if you can unequivocally answer yes. To answer the question, consider some related subquestions such as: Does the message have a subject? Will the recipient at once understand the context and the meaning of the message? Will the recipient immediately know who it's from? Will the recipient know the reply address? If you can answer affirmatively to all of these, you are well on your way to being a seasoned e-mail user.

Managing Your Mail

Once you start using e-mail regularly, you will discover that both your In and Out mailboxes can quickly grow in size. When you try to locate a message sent either to you or by you, say, a few months ago, you'll likely have to wade through many different messages appearing in one big, long list. That's the point when you'll have to do something about your mailboxes! From time to time you should go through your mail and delete all the messages that you know you'll never need to refer to again. If you delete a message by mistake or have second thoughts, fortunately the message is not lost, because Eudora places deleted messages in the *Trash* mailbox. As long as a message is in trash, you can always go there and transfer it back. Messages remain in trash until you select *Empty Trash* from the *Special* pull-down menu, or until you quit Eudora after turning on *Empty Trash on Quit* in the *Settings* dialogue box.

Next, you should create specialized mailboxes and file all of the messages you want to keep into these. You should begin by looking over the list of mail you want to keep. Then create some logical general categories and subcategories, if you wish, for the subjects of your mail. I find that my mail falls into four main categories:

- "personal," including messages from friends and relatives and employment-related matters;
- "administrative," including messages about faculty meetings, university regulations, and all matters related to my position;
- "professional," including messages from students, correspondence about my teaching, research, and professional development; and
- "miscellaneous," for all matter that I cannot classify into any of the above.

Within each of the main categories, I have subcategories. For instance, in the "professional" category, I have subcategories on teaching, research, and professional development. When these categories became too large and diverse, I started making subsubcategories. Under "professional development" I made categories for messages that people send me about interesting new Internet sites, announcements about professional-development workshops and conferences, and messages about professional-development projects I'm undertaking.

Creating mailboxes is effortless in Eudora. From the *Window* pull-down menu, select *Mailboxes*, click on *New* in the Mailboxes window, enter the name of the mailbox you want to create, and then click on *OK*. The mailbox is then added to the list. Below you can see how I added a mailbox named "professional" to the three existing mailboxes that I already had (see Figure 2–4).

You can see that I also checked the box for *Make it a folder*. When you check this, the mailbox can be subdivided into additional mailboxes. I checked it because I wanted to subdivide my "professional" mailbox into three others: "teaching," "research," "professional development." When I created these, I followed exactly the same procedure except that I did not check the *Make it a folder* box. Afterwards, if you are not happy with the name of your mailbox, or if you want to get rid of one, you can highlight the name of the mailbox in the window and click on either the *Rename* or *Remove* button.

Once you have your mailboxes created, you are then ready to file your incoming and outgoing mail into the appropriate mailbox. To do this highlight the message you want to file in either the In, Out, or Trash mailboxes, then from the *Transfer* pull-down menu choose the name of the mailbox you want your message to be filed in. As soon you release your mouse button, the file is transferred.

Other mail programs may not be as convenient as Eudora for managing your mail. Some may even require you to go outside of the program and create your own folders or

Figure 2–4

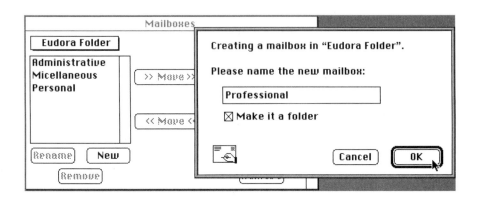

directories in which to save your messages. Regardless of the e-mail package you use, you should develop the habit early on of filing your mail into categories that make the most sense to you. When you develop your own personal network of e-mail contacts around the globe, the rewards gained from a well-managed filing system will be well worth the small investment in time.

3

Accessing Internet Resources with a Web Browser

In addition to being able to use e-mail software effectively, in taking control of your professional development with the Internet, you will also need to be able to use a Web browser, to access the plethora of resources on the Net suitable for professional development. Contrary to what the name implies, a Web browser is a tool that allows you to access much more than World Wide Web documents. With a Web browser you can also conveniently access FTP, Telnet, and Gopher resources, as well as read Internet news.

In this chapter, I'll explain how to access Internet resources with the browser Netscape Navigator. For simplicity and because it's common practice, I'll refer to Netscape Navigator simply as "Netscape." Even if you don't use Netscape, the concepts and principles in this chapter will be equally applicable to other popular Windows or Macintosh browsers, such as Mosaic and Microsoft's Internet Explorer.

Navigating with Netscape

With the advent of the Web, the metaphor of "navigating" through the "sea of information" available on the Internet has become commonly used. What people mean when they talk about "navigating" is simply "getting to where they want to go" on the Internet. To do this, they "point" their browser to a specific resource by entering in its URL (the Internet address of a resource), clicking on a hypertext link, or clicking on the back or forward arrows of their Web browser. In this section, I'm going to describe these and other techniques for navigating the Internet with Netscape. As you read this section,

Figure 3–1

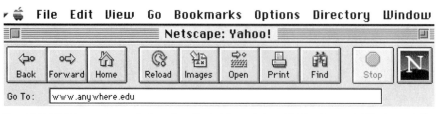

you may wish to refer to the screen shot in Figure 3–1 of Netscape's pull-down menu list, the toolbar, and the *Go to* line (known as the location field).

What Do the Back and Forward Arrows Really Do?

Even after a cursory use of Netscape you'll have discovered the navigation arrow buttons at the top left of the toolbar. They allow you to jump backward and forward from the page you are currently viewing. At first glance this concept seems simple enough to understand. But in practice, you may be surprised by what Netscape really does when it takes you backward or forward.

To understand the function of these commands, select *History* from the *Window* pull-down menu. You will see a window, shown in Figure 3–2, that provides a record of the sites you've recently visited. The most recent page you've viewed is at the top of the list, while the very first page you viewed is at the bottom of the list. Now suppose you clicked on "Yahoo!" (about halfway down the History list), and the clicked on the *Go to* button. The Yahoo! page would appear on your screen. Now if you clicked on Netscape's back arrow, you would be taken to "Welcome to Europe Online"; and if you clicked on the forward arrow, you would be taken to "Yahoo!—Education." Thus "forward" really means "take me to the next highest page on the History list" and back means "take me to the next lowest page on the History list." Note that if you are at the top of the list, clicking on the forward arrow will not do anything; similarly, if you are at the bottom of the list, the back arrow will not do anything.

While navigating from one page to another via the back and forward arrows, you have the choice of either closing the History window or leaving it open. I suggest closing it to prevent your screen from becoming too cluttered. On the other hand, you may wish to leave it open for easy reference.

Figure 3–2

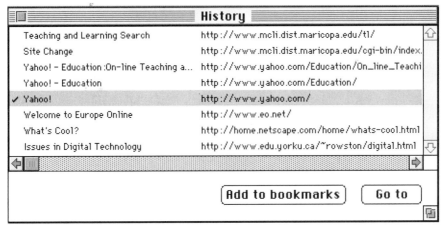

You will find that in Netscape, as with other Web browsers, there's almost always more than one way to accomplish a task. In addition to the back and forward arrows or the *Go to* command on the History list, here are three more ways you can navigate backward and forward:

• Hold the mouse button down for a moment anywhere on the page you are viewing. A handy pop-up menu will appear that offers you a choice of either of the back and forward commands.

• Select *Back* or *Forward* from the Go pull-down menu.

• Look further down on the *Go* pull-down menu and you'll see a list of the names of the sites you have already visited. Select any of these sites and you will immediately link to it. Unlike the History window, which has the entire record of where you've visited since you last started Netscape, the *Go* menu only lists recent sites you visited.

Getting to a Specific Location

When someone tells you about a great Web site you must visit and gives you the address (say it's *http://www.anywhere.edu*), here are three ways to get there with Netscape.

First, you can go to the *File* pull-down menu and select *Open Location*. You'll then see a dialogue box. When you enter the location (*www.anywhere.edu*) and click on *Open*, Netscape will take you to that site. It is optional to enter *http://* protocol prefix;

however, if you had wanted to go to a location other than a Web site, you must type the complete URL. The other valid URL protocol prefixes are:

gopher:// (to connect to Gopher resources)

news: (to connect to specific newsgroups)

telnet:// (to remotely log on to UNIX computers)

TN3270:// (to remotely log on to IBM mainframe computers)

The bottom two protocols—Telnet and TN3270—require special "helper" software in order to be linked to Netscape. I'll explain helper software later in this chapter. You should note that *news:* is not followed by the double forward slashes ("//").

The second way is to click on the *Open* button on the toolbar. You will then see the identical dialogue box and you can proceed in exactly the same way.

A third way to get to a specific location is to enter the URL directly in the *Go to* line immediately beneath Netscape's toolbar and then press return on your keyboard. You don't need to enter the *http://* prefix using this method either.

Using Bookmarks

Keeping track of where you've been is one of the greatest challenges you'll face when navigating the Internet. As I mentioned above, the History window keeps a record of the sites you've visited during the current session only. Once you quit Netscape and restart it, the History window is cleared. Fortunately, you don't have to make a manual note of the sites you wish to return to because of the bookmarks feature. Bookmarks are analogous to folding over the corner of the page on a book you're reading when you find something interesting that you might want to revisit.

Bookmarks are very easy to create in Netscape. When you visit a site you wish to mark, simply go to the *Bookmarks* pull-down menu while you are at the site and select *Add Bookmark*. You'll then see the title of the page added to the pull-down menu. Netscape obtains the title from the name that appears in the title bar for the page. Any time you want to return to the page, go back to the *Bookmarks* pull-down menu and select the name of the site. Another way to create bookmarks is to go to the History window, click anywhere on the line containing the name and address for the page you want to mark, and then click on the *Add to bookmarks* dialogue box.

Once you get into the habit of creating bookmarks, you'll soon discover that your list of markers has grown exceedingly long. You'll also find that you can't remember what page many bookmarks refer to because their titles often don't bear any relation to the contents of the page they are marking. Fortunately, Netscape allows you to group your bookmarks into logical categories and rename them. These tasks are accomplished by selecting *Bookmarks* from the *Window* pull-down menu. When you do this you'll see a window like the one in Figure 3–3 containing all your bookmarks. Also notice that the menu bar across the top changes from Netscape's standard menu bar to a new one containing only *File, Edit, Item,* and *Window.*

In order to deal with your long list of bookmarks, the first thing you'll probably want to do is delete any unwanted bookmarks. To delete a bookmark, click once on it, go to the *Edit* pull-down menu, and select *Delete Bookmark.* When you scroll down your list you'll likely encounter some bookmarks that you no longer recognize. Double click on any of these and you'll link to the site directly (provided you are presently connected to the Internet). If you want to change the name of a bookmark, click on the line containing it and select *Edit* from the *Item* pull-down menu. You'll see another window like the one in Figure 3–4. You can then replace the name with one that you prefer. You can also add a note about the site in the description field of the bookmark. Once you finish this, click on *OK* and the bookmark is updated.

Once you're happy with the contents of your bookmark list, you'll want to organize them into logical categories. You'll recall that when discussing how to manage e-mail messages, I suggested that you create mailboxes for personal, administrative, professional, and miscellaneous matters. You may wish to give your groupings of bookmarks

Figure 3–3

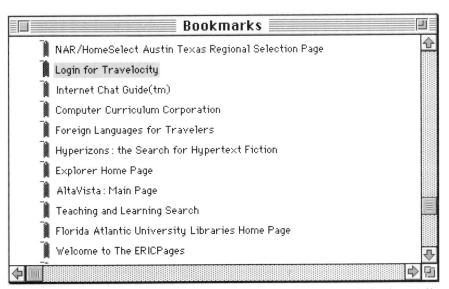

Figure 3–4

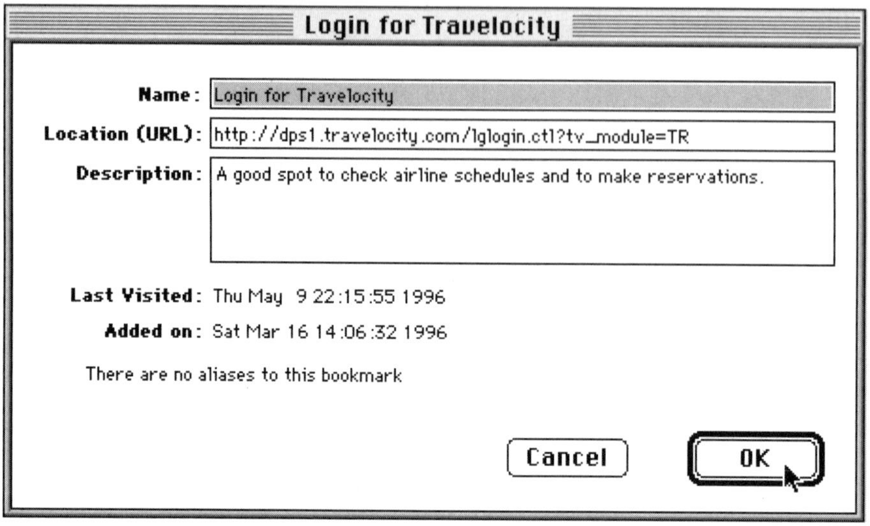

Login for Travelocity

Name : Login for Travelocity

Location (URL) : http://dps1.travelocity.com/lglogin.ctl?tv_module=TR

Description : A good spot to check airline schedules and to make reservations.

Last Visited : Thu May 9 22:15:55 1996

Added on : Sat Mar 16 14:06:32 1996

There are no aliases to this bookmark

Cancel   OK

---

the same titles. By doing so, you'll have continuity between how you organize your mail and your bookmarks, thus making it easier to remember what kinds of items you've placed in each category. For illustration, I'll assume that you want to make a bookmark category entitled "professional development."

To create a new category, select *Insert Folder* from the *Item* pull-down menu. You'll see a dialogue box that is identical to the one above except that there is no space to add a URL. Enter the name of the folder (professional development) and a few words to describe its content and click *OK*. Your new folder is now created at the top of the bookmark list.

You can then file all of your "professional development" bookmarks into the new folder by selecting them from the main list and dragging them into the folder. Double click on any folder and you will see the bookmarks it contains. Continue sorting your bookmarks until you have removed all of them from your main list.

You can create subfolders, too, for any of your main bookmark folders. To do this, select the folder in which you want a subfolder and follow the same procedure for creating a new folder.

After you close the Bookmarks window, you will see the names of your new bookmark folders under the *Bookmarks* pull-down menu. Inside of them will be all of the sorted bookmarks and any subfolders you created. If you faithfully follow this process, in the end you will have a very efficient way of returning to sites of interest to you.

Netscape and the Browser Metaphor

Metaphors about the Internet abound because of the need to make its technical jargon and abstract concepts understandable to the ordinary computer user. By comparing the use of Netscape to browsing through a book, you may find this software tool easier to understand. Think of the Web as a book that you happen to open at a random page. From that page you can thumb backward and forward just as Netscape's navigation arrows move you from page to page. If you jotted down the numbers of the pages you looked at, you'd have a record of what you saw, which is similar to Netscape's History window. If you wanted to reread a passage, you would likely look at your list of page numbers and flip to that page. With Netscape you'd do the same by clicking on a page title in the History list or the *Go* menu. If there were a page in the book you wanted to return to next time you picked it up, you'd fold over the page corner. Netscape's bookmarks are for the same purpose. Finally, if there were a particular topic you wanted to read about, you'd look for the relevant page number in the table of contents or index and open the book to that page. Similarly, with Netscape, if you find out about a site you want to visit, you'd click on Netscape's *Open* button and enter in the site's URL. Keep this metaphor in mind the next time you use Netscape and you'll find navigating the Web as easy as thumbing through a book.

Retrieving the Contents of Web Pages

During your professional-development activities, there'll be times when you want to save to your computer's hard drive all or part of the contents of a Web page for future reference, so that you don't have to connect to the Internet every time you want to access the information. There are several ways to accomplish this. Throughout the following explanation, I'll assume you are connected to the Internet and have the information you wish to retrieve appearing on your screen.

Using the *Save As* Command

The *Save as* command allows you to save the entire text of a Web page to your hard drive. Select *Save as* from the *File* pull-down menu. You'll then be prompted with the choice of two formats: *text* or *source*. If you select *text*, you will be prompted as to what folder or directory on your hard drive you want to save the text of the page in and what file name you want to give it. After you provide the appropriate information and click on *Save*, the page will be saved on your hard drive. From then on, to view the contents, you must open the file with your word processor. Note that when you select the text option, all graphics, pictures, and special formatting of the original page are lost.

If you select *source* instead of *text*, you save the page in a file format known as HyperText Markup Language (HTML). This is a format that contains codes which tell browsers how to display Web pages on computer screens. By saving the page as source, you will be able to preserve the special formatting of the text of the Web page you are viewing; however, you still will not be able to save the pictures and graphics. To save the page in source format, follow exactly the same steps as above. To view the page, you need to use Netscape, but you do not need to be connected to the Internet. Simply select *Open File* under the *File* pull-down menu, locate the file on your hard drive, and click on *Open*. You will then see the page fully formatted the way you saw it online.

Copying Text

Sometimes you may wish to retrieve only a portion of the text of a Web page. Rather than using the *Save as* command, highlight with your mouse the portion of the text you want and choose *Copy* from Netscape's *Edit* pull-down menu. This will save the text temporarily in your computer's clipboard. Now open a new or existing document in your word processor and click on *Paste* from your word processor's *Edit* pull-down menu. The text will then appear in your word processor; however, you will lose the special formatting of the Web page with this process too.

Retrieving Images

Images on Web pages have to be retrieved separately from text. Click your mouse on the image you want to retrieve and continue to hold down the button. A menu will pop up offering two relevant choices: *Save this Image as* and *Copy this Image*. The first choice will save the image on your hard drive after you provide a file name and select a directory. To view the image afterward, you'll need to have graphics software on your computer that can accept either GIF or JPEG formats (the formats of almost all Web images). Some word processors may allow you to import these picture-file formats into a document too. The second choice on the pop-up menu copies the image to your computer's clipboard. Once you've done this, you can open a new or existing document in your word processor or graphics package. Select *Paste* from the *Edit* pull-down menu, and the image will appear in the document.

Mailing Pages

If, when you're working on a computer that's not your own, you discover a Web page you wish to keep, Netscape allows you to mail yourself a copy of the page. You might also want to use Netscape's mail feature to send a copy of an interesting page to a colleague.

Figure 3–5

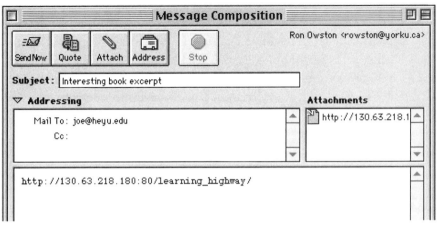

To mail a page, select *Mail Document* from the *File* pull-down menu while viewing the page you wish to send. You will then see a *Message Composition* form with the URL of the page already entered into the message area (Figure 3–5).

You can add any additional text in the message area. Next enter a word or two in the *Subject* line to describe the contents of the message, and enter either your own e-mail address or that of the person you want to send the page to in the *Addressing* box. Double check that the address is correct, then select *Send Now*. Netscape will send the text of the page directly from the Web site you are viewing to the address you gave. The message will arrive at its destination as unformatted text and will appear exactly as it would have if you had saved it to your local hard drive as text using the *Save as* command.

Customizing Netscape

As soon as Netscape is installed it is fully functional for everyday Web browsing. After you've gained confidence and experience with Netscape, however, you may wish to customize some of its settings and expand its viewing capabilities. When you are ready to do this, take a detailed look at *General Preferences* in the *Options* pull-down menu. You'll see numerous items whose settings can be modified. The items are grouped together on seven pages. Each page can be accessed by clicking on the page heading tab. I will explain only those settings that you're most likely to want to change. However, I encourage you to experiment with the preferences settings, until you have Netscape operating exactly the way you wish.

Changing the Appearance of Netscape

The *Appearance* settings page shown in Figure 3–6 is the first one you'll see under *General Preferences*. There are two items here that you may wish to change. First is the *Home Page Location*. This is the location that you will be taken to each time you start up Netscape and connect to the Internet, or whenever you click on the *Home* icon. If it hasn't been changed since Netscape was first installed on your computer, the URL of Netscape Corporation will appear in the field. You can enter any valid URL in this field. Many people use the URL of their institution or that of their personal home page, and you may wish do so as well.

The second appearance setting you may wish to alter is *Followed Links Expire*. You probably have noticed that when you click on a link to a Web page and then return to the

Figure 3–6

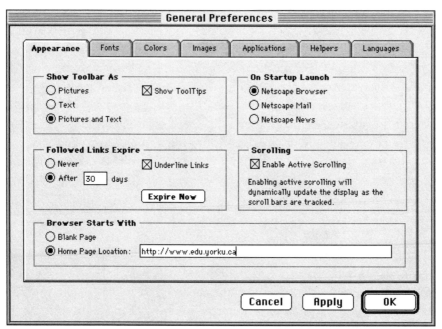

original page, the color of the link changes (for example, from blue to purple). The reason for the color change is to notify you that you've already looked at that link. This is a very handy feature because it's so easy to forget which pages you've viewed. If the exact same link appears on an entirely different page, you'll notice that the color has changed on that page as well. Netscape allows you to set the time when the links change back to their original colors by making the appropriate selection: never, after a set number of days, or immediately. Although thirty days is the default setting, you may wish to reduce the time to remind you to revisit key sites, or increase it if you're spending more than a month researching a topic and don't want to waste time revisiting sites you've already seen.

Selecting Applications

On the *Applications* page (see Figure 3–7), you'll notice four settings. They are important, so you should make sure you fully understand their function. The first two enable you to connect to specific kinds of Internet sites, the third is for viewing source documents (I'll explain these below), and the fourth helps you keep track of downloaded software.

Some Internet sites, such as libraries and specialized databases, require a Telnet or TN3270 connection. Earlier in this chapter, you saw that both of these were valid protocols in forming a URL. When you want to connect to a site that requires either of these protocols, however, you need to do more than simply enter the URL and expect Netscape to connect to the site. In addition, you must have Telnet or TN3270 software installed on your computer and you must tell Netscape where the software can be found on your hard drive. The software is normally supplied by your Internet service provider or it can be downloaded for free on the Internet (below I will describe how to download software). To tell Netscape where the software is on your hard drive, click on *Browse* beside *Telnet* or *TN3270 Applications*, and locate the directory or folder where the software is installed. Once you find the software, highlight its name with your mouse and click on *Open*.

The third setting, called *View Source*, tells Netscape what software to use when you select *Document Source* from the *View* pull-down menu. This menu item allows you to see the HTML coded version of a page that you are viewing. You are likely to want to choose this item only if you are learning how to create your own Web page and want to see how someone else achieved a certain effect using HTML. You have two choices for this setting: you can view the document within Netscape's window by checking *Use Netscape*, or you can use any word processor that you have on your computer by clicking on *Browse* and following the same procedure as described above.

The last setting on the page allows you to choose exactly where on your hard drive you want Netscape to store downloaded software. You may even wish to create a separate directory or folder called Downloads for this purpose. To set the directory, click on *Browse*, locate the folder or directory you want to use, and click on *Select*.

Figure 3–7

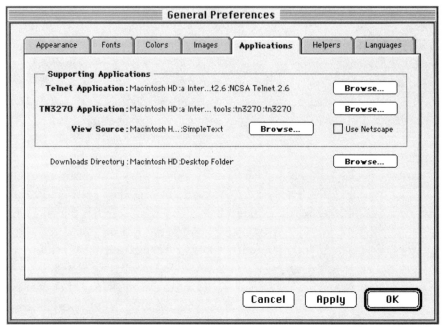

The downloading process itself is effortless with Netscape. When you encounter a link on a Web page that tells you that it is for downloading software, you simply click on the link and the software is downloaded.

Setting Up Helpers

When Netscape encounters a sound, image, or video file or a compressed file on the Internet that it cannot display within its own window or process itself, it launches a *helper* software program to do the job. On the other hand, there are certain kinds of files that Netscape can display or process, but only with the assistance of another kind of program called a *plug-in*. The *Helpers* preference page (see Figure 3–8) is for telling Netscape which helper or plug-in program to use when it encounters one of these files.

Before showing you how to set up helpers and plug-ins, here are three examples of helpers:

- PKUNZIP (Windows) or Stuffit Expander (Macintosh), to translate and decompress downloaded software

Figure 3–8

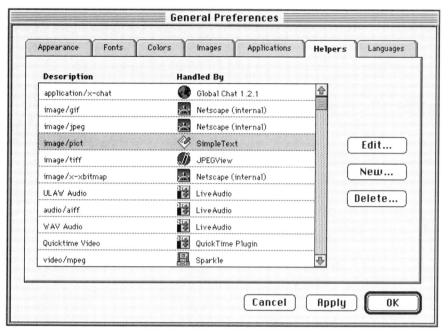

- Global Chat (Macintosh and Windows), to conduct IRC (chat) sessions
- Sparkle (Macintosh), to view movies in the commonly found MPEG format.

Telnet and TN3270 software applications are often referred to as helpers, too, but as you saw above, Netscape has a separate page for referencing them. Some examples of plug-ins are:

- Shockwave, which lets you view animation created with Macromedia's Authorware software tool
- Acrobat Reader, which lets you view, navigate, and print Portable Document Format (PDF) files
- RealAudio, which allows the playback of sound without waiting for the whole sound file to be downloaded

Most helpers and plug-ins are available for free, although some are sold commercially. At Netscape's Web site (*http://www.netscape.com*), you can download most of the available free helpers and plug-ins.

When you view the Helpers preference page, on the left side you see a list of names of different file types frequently found on the Internet. Immediately to the right is a list of names of helpers or plug-ins that Netscape uses to handle the adjacent file type. When you install plug-ins they are normally automatically added to these columns, so that you don't have to do anything further. If the column is not automatically modified, then the software developer will often provide step-by-step instructions on what to do.

Unlike plug-ins, helpers almost always require manual setup. Suppose you want to change or install a helper to view image files in PICT format. First, you need to determine what software program will allow you to view this kind of file. If you don't already know this, you need to find out either by trial and error or by reading the documentation for software you think might do the job. (In this illustration, I chose SimpleText for the Macintosh.) Then, in the Helpers preference window, click on the line containing *image/pict* and click again on *Edit*. You will next see a dialogue box which prompts you to locate and select the software program on your hard drive that you want to use to view the image. Once you have selected it, click on *OK*, and the setting is modified.

Admittedly, setting up the Helper page is somewhat tedious; however, you need to get used to doing it if you want to take full advantage of the software available to extend Netscape's capabilities.

Languages

Some Web sites make their pages available in several different languages. You can tell Netscape to automatically request the page in another language, if it is available. This could be a very handy feature if you are a foreign-language teacher and want practice reading in that language.

To set up Netscape to request another language version of a page, you only have to select the language you want from a list on the *Language* preference page. You can even select more than one language in order of priority (e.g., display the French version if it's available, otherwise display the Spanish version). You should note, however, that only a relatively small number of sites publish their pages in more than one language.

Part II

Creating an Action Plan

Planning is the key to successful use of the Internet for professional development. Pam Lloyd, a fifth-grade teacher at Kincaid Elementary in the Anchorage, Alaska, school district, should know. Every day she logs on to the Internet for one to two hours and deals with approximately two hundred e-mail messages! Here's what Pam says about planning and professional development using the Internet.

> As technology develops at an exponential rate, I find myself increasingly excited, exhilarated, and eager to integrate technology into my classroom and my professional life. But I feel it's essential to start with a plan. I continually set goals, keep lists, and think about my future. I always share my goals with my administrator, colleagues, and parents, because I believe the more you rehearse personal aims with others, the more you are likely to achieve them. I am a list maker, and I love to cross off accomplished tasks. During the year I revisit this list, to see what I have accomplished and reassess what it is I need to continue to work on to maintain my personal and professional growth.
>
> I currently belong to approximately twenty mailing lists. From my participation in these, I feel I have learned so much from other educators around the world regarding

professional development, lesson planning, technology tips, and more. This network of people has perhaps been the single most important motivator for me to learn more, do more, and teach more using technology as a tool.

When I first began to use the Internet, I became frustrated and felt like I wasn't getting the answers I was searching for. I was just blindly surfing. Then I learned how to use search engines and how to differentiate between good information and information that was questionable. Now I teach my students how to find credible information, teaching them to look at the Web site address or URL and always to check to see who is writing the information. I spend countless hours researching topics and building treasure hunts, activity pages, and lists of sites for my students, to teach them to be successful researchers.

Much of my professional development has come from online courses. My first online course was through the University of Alaska. Class participants were from all over Alaska and some parts of the western United States. We were all on a mailing list with two instructors who served as moderators. We learned about basic Internet concepts and tools, and discussed the issues of privacy and federal regulations regarding the Internet. It was an extremely interesting course. I enjoyed being able to learn from my home, at my convenience. Although I never personally met the instructors, I was in direct communication with them through e-mail. Currently I am enrolled in several online courses, including Building Your Home on the Web (Introduction to HTML), Graphic and Design Shop, and Fun Things to Do on the Net, which are offered free of charge by Spectrum Virtual University.

As for my future, I'm even planning to teach online. I am pursuing an opportunity to offer an online course for students in grades four through eight, which will include coursework in safely and responsibly searching the Internet, Internet projects, worldwide communication through e-mail "key pals," and passion research projects. Through a year-long class with other educators in our district, I helped develop and write the curriculum for a multimedia course for the University of Alaska at Anchorage and Alaska Pacific University that I hope will be offered online next year as a credit course.

Overall, I believe the Internet has given me the means for sharing my knowledge as well as learning from others in a risk-free environment. I have never been afraid to learn new things. Perhaps that is my greatest gift as a teacher—to be able to model life-long learning.

While your professional development needs to be carefully planned and thought out, you also need to be flexible so that you can take advantage of unforeseen opportunities that may arise. Art Wolinsky's (*awolinsk@concentric.net; http://dune.srhs.k12.nj.us*) remarkable career is testimony to this.

In September of 1995 I was teaching Multimedia Production in the unlikely setting of a small trailer at Southern Regional, an overcrowded grades seven-to-twelve rural regional school district in South Jersey. I had no Internet experience whatsoever. Today, I'm called an Internet expert and I'm a nationally known speaker. I say that not out of hubris, but out of amazement. It is not a place I planned to be, but as I look back over thirty years of teaching I can now see how I arrived.

Accidents, planning, and luck have had equal roles in getting me here. It started in 1979 when a message was mistakenly delivered to my mailbox. It told me of a program which offered a two-week loan of a TRS-80 computer to teachers. Within hours of getting my hands on the computer and typing my first three-line program, I was hooked. I began taking workshops, reading, and "playing." I wrote programs and lessons designed to put the power of the computer to work in the classroom.

Three years later I logged on to my first bulletin board system (BBS). This put me in touch with a whole new world and opened my eyes to online collaboration. I began participating in professional BBSs run by the National Education Association (NEA), the state department of education, and other organizations. Another accident (double hernia) put me out of work for six weeks. I took the time to create the state's first educational BBS. Later, I wrote grants for the use of computers to promote basic skills and adult education and established a portable computer sign-out program for our school.

In 1989 I discovered multimedia. My online activities made it possible for me to become an expert in a short time. I was participating in an IBM BBS that provided online support for Linkway, their multimedia program. Within two months of getting on the BBS and working daily with the program developers, I wrote a grant to create a program to teach the digestive system. The program opened another door and I became a part-time educational instructional specialist for IBM, and established the East Coast's first multimedia production elective at my school.

Our school went online in April of 1995. I was charged with learning the Internet, training teachers, and writing curriculum for an Internet elective for September. On top of that, I signed up to participate in an eight-week Online Internet Institute (OII) funded by the National Science Foundation (NSF). I began to panic when I realized what I had to accomplish in the next few months. There obviously weren't enough hours in the day.

What happened is a testimony to the power of online collaboration and the potential for real-life problem solving. I immersed myself in online activities and exploration. Rather than simply participate in OII, I felt my best course of action was to become a mentor in the program and lead a group interested in creating online training tools. I connected with Sue Myers, another teacher charged with writing curriculum. We gathered about a dozen other online collaborators and began creating a Web site to teach

Internet basics. The Web site would become the core of the curriculum, would serve as a teacher training tool, and would be the focus of the OII activities. Somehow all of the activities overlapped and complemented one another.

They say ignorance is bliss. I went about the task totally oblivious to the fact that I was getting messages from some of the "giants" of the Internet. Messages from Al Rogers, Gleason Sackman, Melanie Golden, Andy Carvin, Ferdi Serim (OII founder), and others came and went on a daily basis. I conversed with them in total ignorance of their status. As I learned who they were I began to really get a feel for the power of the online community to create systemic change.

By the time September rolled around we had a Web site and project which was testimony to the power of online collaboration and a model for what education should really be about, namely real-life problem solving. The total was far greater than the sum of the parts. In October the curriculum was distributed to about fifty thousand schools as part of a Global School Network CD, and I had unknowingly done something others viewed as a significant achievement.

As a member of OII, I'm engaged in systemic reform and online community-building. I've been invited to participate in national initiatives and forums I never even knew existed. Because of my BBS and multimedia experience, I was prepared to make this type of giant leap, but without question I know that others can make giant leaps within their classrooms and open up a new world to their students too.

I've learned that the Internet is a tool that can shatter the Peter Principle. I feel I have been catapulted about ten levels above my competence, but the unqualified support of the online community helped me rise to levels I never envisioned. Online collaboration was, without a doubt, the most important activity I've undertaken in my career. I would encourage anyone contemplating going online to do so without hesitation. Self-doubt is the greatest obstacle to success. Online participation and the support of the online community will soon remove such doubt and pave the way for success.

4 | How to Develop an Action Plan

Most human-resources development specialists urge that professionals have career-development plans. Their recommendation is based on studies of persons who have demonstrated outstanding success in their chosen field. These people tend to have a vision of where they would like to go with their career, how they're going to reach their goal, and what the signposts are along the way to indicate their progress. A career-development plan puts you in control of your future, rather than letting circumstances dictate the direction your career takes. Of course, a plan by no means guarantees success. What a plan does is increase your chances of having a rewarding career that unfolds according to your ambitions and desires.

The development of a career plan is beyond the scope of this book. However, it is a process that I would strongly encourage any teacher to undergo. If you don't have a career plan, you may wish to look at some of the readings suggested in the appendix of this book, or consult with a human resources counselor in your school district. What this book will do is help you take advantage of the potential of the Internet as a medium to help you grow professionally. Ideally, the professional-development activities you undertake with the Internet should fit within the overall framework of your career plan. If you don't have a career plan, this book may serve to stimulate your interest in developing one.

In this chapter, you will learn how to create a professional-development action plan that incorporates the Internet. An action plan consists of goals you wish to accomplish, strategies or tactics that can enable you to reach your goals, timelines for carrying out these strategies, and a mechanism to monitor your progress. The action plan will form the foundation for all of your professional-development activities on the Internet.

Serendipity or Growth Plan: Which Route to Take?

Although I believe that all professional development should be systematically planned, when you use the Internet as a development tool, the need for planning becomes doubly important. Let's spend a moment to consider why a plan is beneficial.

There is simply too much information available on the Internet to wade through it without a charted course. Imagine the largest library you've ever seen, multiply the number of books in that library many, many times over, and picture all of these books dumped into a pile. This will give you an idea of the vastness and chaos of the Internet. Information and resources are scattered across the globe on hundreds of thousands of computers. No central authority controls what or how information is posted at Internet sites, nor is there any universal scheme for indexing information for search and retrieval.

The World Wide Web makes the task of navigating the Internet somewhat easier by providing hypertext links to information, as you saw in the last chapter. Clicking on these links with your mouse allows you to maneuver seamlessly from one computer to the next, without regard to where the information is physically located. Still, it's easy to get lost in the sea of information, forgetting where you started and your original purpose. Wandering aimlessly, you will have wasted a very precious commodity—your time!

In planning your professional development systematically, you make the best use of the overall time you have available for this activity. Let's say you set aside three hours a week to inquire about an aspect of your teaching that you want to improve. Rather than simply surfing the Internet for three hours, wouldn't your time be better spent if you set yourself guidelines of, say, about an hour to participate in an online forum on the topic, another hour to thoroughly research your topic, and another hour to read the fruits of your research?

I'm not arguing that you should be overly rigid in your online work. There certainly are times when you'll want to follow a link that offers a promising insight into your topic. You may also learn, by chance, that there are dimensions to your topic that you were totally unaware of. This would require follow-up. On the other hand, you may reach a dead end. There may simply be no information or no one available online who can help you with your specific topic. This may force you to alter your line of inquiry or abandon the subject altogether. So you need to have a certain measure of flexibility in your approach.

Overall, your plan sets the direction for your professional development. It contains goals, and strategies to reach them; it weaves the Internet into those strategies; and it is constantly monitored and updated by you as you gain new perspectives.

Creating an Action Plan
1. Set Your Professional-Development Goals

The first step in developing your professional-growth action plan is to set your goals. This will require that you assess your professional needs and priorities for both the near future and the long run. Many schools encourage teachers to develop personal-growth plans or broader career plans, so you may have already articulated your professional-development goals. In that case, you may wish to review them in light of our discussion here to see where the Internet can facilitate your plans. If you haven't set any professional-development goals for yourself, you'll want to begin by asking yourself short-term questions such as:

- What would I like to do better?
- What do I need more information on?
- What areas of my teaching do I need to improve?
- In what areas are my students having difficulty and how can I better deal with those topics?

and long-term questions such as:

- Where would I like to be professionally in six months; twelve months; next year?
- What grade/subjects will I be teaching next year?
- What do I need to do to improve my credentials for salary or professional-advancement purposes?

The short- and long-term goals may or may not relate to one another. For example, you may have difficulty teaching a particular concept and want to find better ways to explain it to students. At the same time, your long-term goal may be to become a school principal. At first glance, these two goals seem unrelated. But the concept that you are having trouble with may be in the same subject area as the graduate courses you would need to take to become a high school department head. Closely related goals offer the added benefit of efficiency. They reinforce each other by focusing your intention into a narrow area. What matters most in deciding upon your goals, however, is whether they truly match what you want to do.

Your goals must also be attainable. One of the worst strategies would be to set a goal and relentlessly pursue it, knowing that you'll likely never achieve it. Although it may seem obvious that your goals should be achievable, you need to assess whether they can be realistically reached in the time you've allotted. If you fail to be realistic, you will become frustrated and feel that your attempts weren't worth the time and effort. The best way to avoid this problem is to consider your goals as directions you'd like to pursue and targets you'd like to meet. You can alter your direction and target when you feel that the path you are following is no longer productive. The rapidly changing and often unpredictable nature of the Internet makes this the only viable strategy to follow. This strategy is not unlike the one Columbus reportedly used to reach North America. His goal was to reach India. He knew the direction in which to head (west) and he followed signposts along the way (compass, birds, sky, waves), but arrived at a different—though nonetheless valuable—landmass (North America) than he expected. You, too, need to have a goal, and along the way, you need to assess the knowledge you accumulate. If you don't reach the exact goal you initially set for yourself, you needn't worry, because what you do achieve may even better match your needs and interests.

To put these ideas in more concrete terms, let's assume you are an eighth-grade teacher. Like many teachers of students at this age, you have difficulty motivating your students to want to learn mathematics. Undaunted, however, you want to meet the challenge head-on and see what you can do to get your students more interested in math and to improve your math teaching in general. You find that one skill which students never seem to pick up well is estimation—the ability to predict distance, area, weight, and volume. Your students, for example, can't judge whether a book you give them weighs a half pound or two pounds, or whether a distant object you point out is one mile or three miles away. So you decide that you would like to:

1. Improve your teaching of estimation skills
2. Seek ways to better motivate your students to want to learn math
3. Improve your overall teaching of math

Goals such as these are workable in terms of their generality and your likelihood of achieving them. They set a direction in which you want to go, starting with improving your teaching of a specific skill, then move to a more general aim of improving student motivation, and conclude with a more ambitious goal of improving your overall math teaching.

2. Link Your Goals to the Internet
Once you've set some reasonably attainable goals, your next task is to develop strategies or tactics that link your goals to the Internet. The method I suggest you follow is to brainstorm questions on possible ways the Internet can help you achieve each goal, and then think of possible strategies you can use to answer the questions. Until you become

fairly familiar with the Internet, you will find this task challenging. The next two sections of this book, Building Virtual Professional Communities and Doing Research on the Internet, will give you a good overall idea of what you can do with the Internet, what's available, and how to find it. When you finish reading these sections, even if you are new to the Internet, you'll be able to return to your plan with fresh ideas about new strategies.

Let's return to the math-teaching goals to illustrate how the Internet could be linked to these goals. You begin by brainstorming questions and strategies on ways the Internet might help. When you brainstorm, think not only of general ideas and strategies, but list actual Internet sites or discussion groups you may have heard about or know for a fact exist. Below are the kinds of questions you might ask. Each question is followed by a possible strategy. You may not understand some of the Internet terminology that I've used. If that's the case, you'll want to revisit these pages after reading the rest of this book.

Goal 1: Improving Teaching of Estimation Skills

Question: What techniques have other teachers used to teach estimation?

Strategy: Post a question on relevant k–12 and mathematics newsgroups to see how other teachers deal with the topic.

Question: Are there any Web pages dealing with estimation?

Strategy: Do a search of Web sites using specific keywords such as "mathematics estimation," "estimating distance, volume, or weight," and "teaching estimation skills."

Question: Is there any computer software available that helps students develop estimation skills?

Strategy: Add "estimation software" to the Web search above. Expand the search to software archives.

Question: Might students be able to articulate problems they've had and were able to overcome?

Strategy: Post a question to a k–12 newsgroup or join a mailing list in which both teachers and students participate. (Caution: don't post a question in a student newsgroup that is clearly social and doesn't welcome adults, especially teachers!)

Goal 2: Motivating Students

Question: How can I make math relate more to students' lives?

Strategy: Search k–12 newsgroup archives to see if this question was ever talked about; post a question on an appropriate newsgroup.

Question: How do I find out what researchers and other authors have said about the topic?

Strategy: Search the ERIC database for articles and research reports on "motivation" and "mathematics"; search the nearest university library for books on the topic.

Question: Does the National Council of Teachers of Mathematics (NCTM) have a Web site that might have resources on this topic?

Strategy: Search the Web for "NCTM" to see if a site exists.

Question: Are there k–12 Web sites that offer papers written on the topic?

Strategy: Do a Web search on "motivation mathematics" and "learning mathematics."

Goal 3: Improving Mathematics Teaching Overall

Question: Are there any virtual communities of mathematics teachers to join? Or do most mathematics teachers take part in general education virtual communities?

Strategy: Ask colleagues (in person or via e-mail), watch for announcements in professional magazines, look through the list of newsgroups and mailing lists to see if any would meet your needs; if you find one, join it and participate.

Question: How can I systematically study my own teaching with the goal of trying to improve it?

Strategy: Do a Web search to see if there are any virtual communities that focus on the "teacher as researcher."

Question: Are there any university mathematics-education courses offered online?

Strategy: Look at the Yahoo Education section under the heading *Online Courses*; search AltaVista for "mathematics education course online."

Question: What Web sites should I monitor regularly for mathematics-education trends, issues, and developments?

Strategy: In your searches of Web sites note any that seem particularly informative; plan on revisiting them regularly for updates.

Once you've generated a list of questions and strategies, you'll want to refine it. There will likely be overlap between questions and strategies for any given goal. In this case, you may want to delete some questions and strategies and combine others, possibly even add some new questions and strategies that come to mind after considering your list as a whole. For example, in our illustration, Web searches seemed to be the best strategy for answering several questions, so you may decide to devote some time searching on keywords that will answer questions about all three goals.

3. Know When You've Reached Your Goals

Once your goals and strategies have been articulated, you will need to give some thought as to how you'll know when you've reached your goals. Your instincts will guide you to some extent. For example, one day while teaching, it may suddenly occur to you that your students are finally beginning to understand the concept of estimation. With this insight, you'll be able to think back to the work you are doing to improve your teaching of this skill and say with satisfaction that you've reached your goal. While insight is certainly helpful, you should still try to develop some concrete indicators for your goals. Not only will these indicators make it easier for you to tell when you've reached your goal, they will contribute to your sense of accomplishment in achieving what you set out to do.

It's not easy to develop good indicators for most goals. Some goals, by their very nature, tend to be fairly general statements, so their indicators will be correspondingly imprecise. The more specific your goals are, the easier your task will be. In our example, you can see that the teaching of estimation (goal 1) is probably easier to assess than improving your math teaching overall (goal 3). Some "experts" recommend that in your action plan you break your goals down into specific, measurable objectives. I do not encourage this approach, because the planning experience and ensuing professional-development activities tend to become mechanistic and burdensome.

Your indicators, for all but the simplest goals, will contain both *direct* and *indirect* evidence that you've accomplished what you set out to do. By direct evidence I mean precise, measurable proof that you've accomplished something. Direct evidence might be such facts as the number of articles and books that you've read on a topic, whether you completed a course in English literature successfully, whether you visited all World Wide Web sites dealing with "special education," or the number of times you participated in an Internet discussion group.

Indirect evidence is obtained by inference or deduction that the measure you are using is a good proxy for the real thing, since the real thing can't be measured directly. For example, if your goals involve improving your classroom practice, your impact on students' intellectual, emotional, or physical growth provides indirect evidence of this. The evidence may be in the form of either your own personal observations or students' results on tests. You must be cautious when using indirect evidence, however, because it is often difficult to make a valid connection between cause (your actions) and effect (student scores). The effects you attribute to yourself could be due to something entirely unrelated to your actions—perhaps even another teacher's actions or a program the students watched on television!

I'll turn again to our three goals to illustrate typical goal indicators.

Goal 1: Improving Teaching of Estimation Skills

Indicators will be that:

- Students will take less time to master the skills in the curriculum
- I will have incorporated into my teaching strategies from other teachers on how they teach estimation
- I will feel more confident when teaching estimation
- I will have participated in a virtual discussion group on the topic
- I will have read several research summaries on the topic

Goal 2: Motivating Students

Indicators will be that:

- I will be able to understand why students were not motivated in my classes
- Students will look forward to math classes more than in the past
- Math test scores overall will have improved
- Students will have become more engaged in their mathematics work
- I will have identified and read the key research on motivation and mathematics

Goal 3: Improving Mathematics Teaching Overall

Indicators will be that:

- I will have successfully completed a mathematics education course
- There will be fewer discipline problems in my math classes
- I will have received a positive assessment of my teaching by my department head
- I will have integrated more real-life applications of math into my curriculum
- I will have increased my enjoyment of teaching

You'll note that I listed five indicators for each goal. This is probably about the right number of indicators for most goals. You should also note that most of the indicators offer only indirect evidence of goal attainment.

4. Develop a Timeline

Now allocate to each of your goals sufficient time to achieve them and create a work schedule. The resulting timeline will help you get going and give you a sense of how you are progressing toward your goals. Suppose you, as the eighth-grade teacher in my example, decide to formally spend four hours a week on all facets of your professional development during the school year. You are probably going to learn sufficient information about the teaching of estimation in about two to three months, if you spend an average of two hours a week on the subject, because it is a relatively straightforward skill. To learn to better motivate students will likely take longer to study because it is a more complex topic, so you'll want to spend several months on that. You may begin by devoting an hour a week to the topic, and more time when you finish your study of estimation. Your goal of improving your math teaching overall will undoubtedly take most of your professional-development time for the remainder of the school year, after you finish your study of motivation. In the end, your overall timeline will likely look something like the following:

Month	Goal 1 Estimation	Goal 2 Motivation	Goal 3 Overall Improvement
September	2 hours/week	1 hour/week	1 hour/week
October	2 hours/week	1 hour/week	1 hour/week
November	2 hours/week	1 hour/week	2 hours/week
December	—	2 hours/week	2 hours/week
January	—	—	4 hours/week
:	—	—	:
:	—	—	:

A table like this can help you visualize when and how you intend to reach your goals. The table will make your goals seem more concrete and achievable. You can easily see, for instance, that if you achieve your first two goals on schedule by January, you might have some time to add new, relatively minor goals to your list, provided you can spare time from goal 3.

Putting It All Together

You are now ready to carry out your professional-development action plan: you've set your goals, you are armed with strategies to reach the goals, you have indicators to tell you when you have accomplished them, and you have a timeline. Now the most exciting part begins. You are ready to log on to the Internet and start pursuing your strategies.

Monitoring Your Progress

While you undertake this quest, you'll need to keep track of your progress. I'll suggest a form for doing this in a moment, but first I'd like to draw your attention to the kind of facts you'll want to record. They include:

• *Internet sites you've visited.* Many sites have very similar names (e.g., Cybermall, Cybrary, Cyberplace) and Internet addresses (e.g., anysite.com, anysite.org, anysite.edu), so when you visit a large number of them, you'll probably quickly forget all but the most interesting ones. Therefore, you should keep a record of the sites visited to avoid wasting time in the future by revisiting them unnecessarily. Since you will probably be doing much of your online work with a Web browser, you should save the addresses of important Web sites as bookmarks.

- *Sites you want to return to—and those you don't.* You'll undoubtedly find sites that are rich in resources pertinent to your topic; others will be disappointing. Again, to avoid wasting time, I recommend that you keep a brief record of your reactions to these sites for future reference. You may even want to informally rate the sites (e.g., "1" excellent/relevant to topic, must revisit; "2" okay, worth going back to if there's time; and "3" don't bother revisiting).

- *Keyword searches you've done, on which search engine, and on what date.* My experience is that if you don't keep track of exactly what keywords you've searched for, you'll end up redoing searches several times on the same words because you have forgotten exactly which words you used earlier. For example, searching for "teaching estimation skills" will give different results than "teaching estimation." You'll also get different results depending on which search engine you use (AltaVista, Lycos, Yahoo, and so on). Therefore, you need to note which search engine you used and the terms you searched for. Finally, keep a record of the date you did the search, as the databases of the major search engines are updated frequently.

- *Time spent on each goal.* You should keep track of the time you spend on each goal, including both time spent online and time spent offline reading downloaded articles or any other reading related to your goals. As you gain more experience using the Internet for your professional development, you may not wish to bother with this; but initially, at least, keep a record. Your record will help you refine your time estimates for future goals and give you a sense of progress.

- *Things to do.* Along the way, you'll no doubt get ideas about issues you want to follow up on or leads on Internet sites that you want to try to locate and visit. Therefore, you'll also want to keep a "To Do" list in your log that notes these items so you don't forget them.

For convenience, keep your word processor (or notepad accessory) open while you are doing your online work. You can then note any of the above items quickly, as well as copy online information from your screen and paste it into your word processor.

Creating an Action-Plan Summary Form

Rather than simply pasting the information on the items above haphazardly into your word processor, you may wish to create an action-plan summary form, such as the one shown in Figure 4–1. Illustrated in this form are the strategies, indicators, and timelines for our eighth-grade mathematics teacher's first goal. In addition to these three information areas, note that there is also a space to record comments on the Internet sites visited, searches carried out, time spent on the goal, and follow-up items. You can follow this format for your own action plan, using one form for each of your goals. Not

Figure 4–1   Action-Plan Summary for Goal Achievement

Goal 1: To Improve Teaching of Estimation Skills

Strategies

Post a question on relevant k–12 and mathematics newsgroups to see how other teachers deal with the topic

Do a search of Web sites using specific keywords such as "mathematics estimation," "estimating distance, volume, or weight," and "teaching estimation skills"

Add "estimation software" to the Web search above. Carry out an Archie and Gopher search for software

Post a question to a k–12 newsgroup or join a mailing list in which both teachers and students participate

Indicators

Students will take less time to master the skills in the curriculum

I will have incorporated into my teaching strategies from other teachers on how they teach estimation

I will feel more confident when teaching estimation

I will have participated in a virtual discussion group on the topic

I will have read several research summaries on the topic

Timeline

September—2 hours/week

October—2 hours/week

November—2 hours/week

Log Comments

Sites visited/dates/comments

Keyword searches/search engines

Time spent

"To do" items

---

only will the form be handy for jotting down notes about your work, but it will serve as a constant reminder of your own strategies, indicators, and timeline.

Regardless of the way you ultimately write up your action plan, I strongly advise that you begin your exploration of the Internet by first thoroughly thinking through what you hope to accomplish, how you'll reach it, when you'll get there, and how you'll know that you've arrived. You will be amply rewarded for the time and effort you put into this process.

Planning for Success

While I have extolled the virtues of using the Internet for professional development, I have not said that the undertaking would be easy. Sustaining the needed drive and initiative to reach your goals will be a major challenge. To keep your motivation high, I suggest you try these strategies.

- *Think positive.* You are taking charge of your growth—not waiting for someone else to decide what you need and when you'll need it. Have confidence in your action plan and in your ability to realize it.

- *Look for feedback.* Learning often occurs in small steps. These steps are consolidated from time to time by big leaps in understanding and sudden insight. You'll know when you've made the big gains, but not the small ones. So start looking for evidence of the small gains. Look back over your action plan from time to time to remind yourself of what you've already accomplished; pause every so often to think about what you're doing differently in the classroom since the time you started your action plan; and listen to yourself to see if the ideas and opinions you express to colleagues, friends, and parents when you talk about your teaching have changed.

- *Set milestones.* Milestones mark progress toward your goals, so consider incorporating some of these into your plan. Set dates for when you expect to complete certain tasks that are necessary for accomplishing your goals. For instance, fix a date to finish your Internet research on a certain topic and set a subsequent date to finish reading the literature you have found on that topic.

Part III

Building Virtual Professional Communities

While direct interaction with colleagues online is a powerful way to grow professionally, another way you can benefit from the Internet is through participating with your students in online projects, particularly those that bring together students and outside experts. Marlene Bourdon-King, a teacher at Malvern Collegiate Institute, and her students participate in Writers in Electronic Residence (WIER), a Canadian online project that links teachers and students with professional authors (*http://www.edu.yorku.ca/wier-home*). Below, Marlene describes the rewards of such an experience.

I began as a dramatic arts teacher in 1974, but ten years later, having returned to university for a year, changed schools, and therefore jobs, I found myself teaching English full time. Gradually, my adoption of "process writing" in my own classes gained me the reputation of the "writing teacher" at Malvern Collegiate Institute, a traditional academic high school in Toronto's southeast community of "the Beaches." In 1988, I began teaching an advanced English course, Writer's Craft, and in the early 1990s, became involved with WIER.

My own computer expertise was virtually nonexistent when I began teaching in the online program. With my department head and I working as partners, we struggled through the technology, adapting as the program and its technology advanced. It was really my students' excitement in sharing their work in an electronic environment, coupled with the unsolicited praise from other schools' students, their teachers, and published Canadian authors online that caused me to think critically about how I was teaching writing. I realized through this positive response that somehow the atmosphere being created in my course was fostering unusual success. This encouraged me to examine the elements of the course that were working well, and to hone those that could use improvement.

Through WIER my students learn to criticize the work of other students in a thoughtful and practical manner. They have learned what constitutes a "useful" response to their own writing, and I encourage, indeed insist, that the response and advice they offer be specific and applicable. The improvement in all my students' (but particularly the weaker ones') ability to articulate critical thought has been astonishing. This clearly carries over into their responses to their peers' writing, but also, most gratifyingly, into the critical eye they aim at their own work. Without the practice and volume of criticism of "anonymous" student writing provided by WIER, that outcome would not likely be produced. As a teacher, my own belief in the value of peer editing has been reinforced and augmented.

The administration of the WIER program can be very time-consuming. Consequently, the ability to chat online with other teachers has, for the most part, eluded me. However, in reading the messages in the "Staff Room" conference and in my few exchanges with other WIER teachers, I feel I have made realizations about what "works" (like sharing my own writing with my students for critical input) and have been able to share what I do with other schools, especially those whose experience is "fledgling."

My most significant learning, I feel, has occurred through the connection with contemporary Canadian writers operating in "Electronic Residence." I have been introduced to many fine writers with whose work I would otherwise have been unfamiliar. In particular, I have learned about writing, and the process of it, from the practitioners themselves, both in sharing and discussing the responses they have sent to my students about their writing, and in online conversations that develop as a result. Canadian author Susan Musgrave has been especially valuable to me as a teacher of writing, because her connection with students is genuine and sincere. She is generous with her advice and subsequent correspondence, and I have learned a great deal from her about all sorts of technical considerations, from how to "show, not tell," to how to work effectively with rhyme in poetry, to how to make the beginning of a story engage the reader immediately, to advising to "write what you know." Learning from the writers has been an incalculable bonus to me as a teacher. Without WIER, it would never have been possible.

5 | Virtual Communities and Professional Development

Throughout the discussion on developing your action plan, I stressed the importance of stating professional-development goals and devising strategies to accomplish them. Now as you begin to explore ways the Internet can help you in your professional development, you will find that it is the pursuit of these goals and strategies—not the technology per se—that will sustain your interest and lead to professional growth. To be sure, the Internet in and of itself is compelling, but it is a means to an end for most of us. Similarly, when you read a book, you don't normally focus on how it was made, the quality of the paper, or the printing process; you focus on the ideas, concepts, and whatever else the pages communicate.

Nevertheless, there is an important distinction between the Internet and other learning technologies: it is an exceedingly more complex, diverse, and rich technology than any other devised to date. Therefore, not only do you need to learn about the possibilities the Internet can offer, but you need to learn how to operate the technology that allows you to tap into this potential. In this section and the next, I will discuss two significant professional-development possibilities the Internet offers—building virtual professional communities and learning through research—and I'll describe how to use the technology that enables them.

I begin with virtual professional communities because they are arguably the most powerful professional-development opportunity made possible by the Internet. First, I'll explain what building a virtual professional community means, describe how virtual professional communities can assist your professional development, and show what learning looks like in a virtual professional community. The remaining chapters in the section will be devoted to describing the kinds of communities available and how you can access them.

What Are Virtual Professional Communities?

From the early days of time-sharing mainframe computers, people communicated by sharing their conversations publicly with others who had access to the same computer. From this method of communication evolved the concept of the electronic bulletin board, analogous to the bulletin board in a supermarket or community center. As networks were established that allowed computers to communicate over great distances, the practice of people talking to each other and sharing their conversations on an electronic bulletin board became firmly entrenched.

Those who participated in these online discussions often felt that they were going to an actual "place," a spot where they could make friends, engage in extended discussions, rant and rave about issues, products, or people, and otherwise share experiences and ideas. Participants also began to describe their experience as being a member of a "virtual community." Now the term *virtual community* is used to describe a group of people who regularly interact online and share common goals, ideals, or values. Howard Rheingold, best-known for his writings and pioneering work at The Well, a San Francisco Bay Area community bulletin board, vividly describes what people do in virtual communities:

> People . . . use words on screens to exchange pleasantries and argue, engage in intellectual discourse, conduct commerce, exchange knowledge, share emotional support, make plans, brainstorm, gossip, feud, fall in love, find friends and lose them, play games, flirt, create a little high art and a lot of idle talk. People in virtual communities do just about everything people do in real life, but we leave our bodies behind. You can't kiss anybody and nobody can punch you in the nose, but a lot can happen within those boundaries. To the millions who have been drawn into it, the richness and vitality of computer-linked cultures is attractive, even addictive. (From *The Virtual Community: Homesteading on the Electronic Frontier* (1993), found at *http://www.well.com/user/hlr/vcbook/index.html.*)

Some critics scoff at the notion of virtual communities, saying that the commitment to shared ideas and values in online discussion groups is ephemeral, that there is no real social contract among participants. Regardless of the question of whether virtual communities are communities in the traditional sense of the word, they fill a need in people for contact and sharing. They are what Ray Oldenburg, author of *The Great Good Place* (1989), calls "third places," places other than work and home, such as cafés, town squares, community centers, beauty shops, taverns, and libraries, where people interact and discuss issues of common concern.

More central to the purposes of this book, virtual communities can provide a rich environment for professional learning and growth. I'll refer to communities of this kind as "virtual professional communities." When you join others regularly online to exchange ideas about teaching, to share successes and disappointments you've had in the classroom, to learn from others, and to help colleagues, you engage in community building. You build a virtual professional community by contributing your individual experiences and expertise to benefit the collective knowledge and wisdom of the group.

How Virtual Professional Communities Can Help You

At the beginning of this book I stated that being able to share your ideas and experiences with colleagues, reflect on them, and then modify your classroom practice is considered by many to be one of the best routes to professional development and growth. Virtual professional communities offer a means for you to engage in this kind of activity on a global scale. Beyond this, there are compelling reasons why you may wish to become involved in virtual professional communities, which I'll describe below.

Varied Learning Opportunities

Virtual professional communities provide a way for you to seek help immediately when the need arises: a student in your classroom suddenly begins to act abnormally because of a family situation and you want to know what you can do to help; the approach you're using to teach a particular concept just doesn't seem to work anymore and you want suggestions for other teaching strategies; or you've been assigned a student teacher by the principal and are uncertain how to proceed. These are just three examples of potential situations you may find yourself in, where you want help immediately. Turning to a virtual professional community is certainly one strategy to deal with these learning needs.

On the other hand, virtual professional communities are not limited to helping with immediate learning. They offer the possibility of long-term, deep exploration of problems and issues affecting your practice. For example, you and your online colleagues may all be teaching the same grade or subject. Over the course of a school year, you can compare and contrast your experiences and incorporate into your own practice techniques suggested by others.

Support for Your Work

Teachers from time to time experience themselves as "outsiders," finding little respect and support from the public or other professionals. The profession is frequently made the scapegoat when education costs spiral or standards decline. Joining a virtual professional community can provide you with a support group of like-minded individuals, all of whom are struggling to improve themselves so that they can better educate their students. Members will recognize and respect what you do and bring dignity and validation to your work, when otherwise you might feel demoralized and insecure.

Flexible and Responsive

Virtual professional communities rarely have pre-set agendas. They respond immediately to members' needs. If you have a burning question or issue to raise, you are almost never ruled out of order. There is just about always someone to offer help or guidance. Moreover, they provide an antidote to the rigidity that characterizes many professional-development approaches today.

Varied in Topic and Culture

The variety in topics discussed by virtual professional communities is remarkable: from anthropology to zoology and all areas you're likely to think of in between. Even if there is not a community now discussing your area of interest, you can create one quite easily. Besides varying in topic, you'll find that the culture of virtual professional communities differs significantly too. Some are formal, others are laid back; some require a moderator to read and approve your submission before it is posted, others are free-for-alls; some encourage you to stick closely to the chosen theme or topic, others are so wide-ranging you wonder how they got their original names; and while some have thousands of regular participants, others count only a handful among their membership. Therefore, with some effort, you will undoubtedly be able to find a community that will match your interests and preferred style of learning.

What Learning Is Like in Virtual Professional Communities

Learning in online communities takes many forms. It might be a sudden insight triggered by a community member's response, being given the answer to a question that has long puzzled you, being won over by a debate and discussion about an issue, experiencing a shift in point of view or a gradual coming to terms with an issue that you care about over an extended period of time. What is most important about learning in virtual professional communities is that, as a result of your interaction with peers, you "construct" your own understanding about issues, concepts, and practices that concern you.

Recently, I witnessed a vivid example of a beginning teacher, who I'll call Tina, constructing her own understanding about an issue she was deeply concerned about—censorship on the Internet. She did this as a direct result of interaction online with her peers in a summer graduate education course I taught. The course was conducted largely via online conferencing, with teachers meeting online daily for a month. Close relationships were formed, as were commitments to the process of learning online and to improving individual classroom practice.

Tina began on July 23 by expressing her view that censorship is essential if we are to protect children. She was responding to another teacher's suggestion that individuals should be responsible for determining what they can or cannot read or view.

> In thinking about the censorship issue I feel that . . . if censorship comes from within the individual person or individual family groups, we end up being surrounded by a host of offensive and damaging materials. . . . Our society allows people to prey upon the innocent, the naive. The government is an extension of me and I want protection for me and my family from things like pornography. Surely we can come up with some consensus that this stuff [offensive materials on the Internet] is not good for anyone and find ways to control it. . . . I still say that responsibility and freedom must go hand in hand.

Two other participants responded to Tina; one pointed out the need for freedom of expression in society, the other dealt with the impracticality of censorship given the workings of the Internet. Tina began to shift her view about the feasibility and advisability of censorship the following day, July 24, when she said

> I've accepted the fact that the Net can't really be controlled, since it is worldwide. Censorship is totally unworkable and instead threatens some of our rights. We, therefore, must work together for other options. . . . By working together as only people in a free country can, I think mutually satisfying solutions will be found.

Tina, however, seemed to remain ambivalent. She realized that it was not technically practical to impose a global censorship scheme and enforce it. On the other hand, she held out hope that people could come together and find "solutions" to the dissemination of offensive materials.

Over the next two weeks, debate and discussion continued among her peers. Some saw the installation of filtering software that allowed children limited access to the Web as a good solution to the problem. Others advocated open access. One participant said that no amount of filtering would work—that it was the responsibility of adults to educate children to make moral judgments about what's right and wrong. That comment provoked a change in heart on the issue in Tina, who on August 8 said:

> I started out believing fully in censorship of the Net with a belief based more on ignorance than anything else. Your statement says it all. We have to allow children to build morals in their minds, otherwise when they are finally released from the filtering machines there won't be anything there but a vacuum.

Tina was now convinced that censorship was not the way to deal with offensive material on the Internet. She then set out the next day, August 9, to tell others about her revelation and convince those that favored censorship that it was not a workable solution to the problem.

> I hope that there isn't anyone [in the conference] who still feels that censorship is possible. I ran across this little piece about the nature of the Net in an article on Singapore's censorship. I think the wording eliminates any doubts about the [feasibility] of censorship. [Tina quotes from an article describing how the Internet was designed to resist nuclear attack by dynamically rerouting traffic around damaged links.] Who would have thought that the cold war would have given birth to such a monumental creation that would revolutionize the world? Ironically, out of . . . the cold war rises the phoenix of a global world.

Initially, Tina had not adequately thought through her position on the issue of censorship. Her instinctive reaction was that children need to be protected. She was then challenged by her peers to confront her opinions. She became informed about the various dimensions of the problem and finally concluded that, while attempts may be made to limit children's access to the Internet, the best protection for them in the long run lies in teaching them about making moral judgments. It is evident that the members of Tina's virtual community provided her with an opportunity to reflect on her own ideas and arrive at a more solid position on the issue.

Other students in the course found that professional development took on an entirely new meaning for them once they were given the freedom to explore the Internet and share their findings with colleagues in online conferences. Witness Hilda, a midcareer elementary teacher.

> I have never enjoyed learning as much as I have [in this program]. . . . Learning is taking on a new dimension as I construct knowledge with my colleagues. I can't articulate

in words how different this learning feels. Much of it seems embedded in a childlike curiosity. My experience must be similar to how a young child feels when he takes his first step, says his first word, and so on. . . . There is an awakening at every turn, a real sense of wonder and adventure.

Added to this excitement is the opportunity to communicate with others in an online conference at times that best suit you, not when a schedule dictates. Virginia, a high school English teacher, reinforced this position when she responded to another teacher in the course whose newfound interest had had a stimulating effect:

> I also could not sleep the other night. All the new and exciting thoughts were running through my head and I got up and turned on the computer until after 3:00 A.M. Had I known you were up too . . . we could have had a chat.

But she later added that, however attractive online learning is, for her, it would never be a substitute for traditional methods:

> As far as returning to a traditional course is concerned, I don't think I'll ever tire of "curling up with a good book" and having face-to-face discussions about it, but just saying that I will miss the Net research and online conferencing is a gross understatement.

Online work benefits from a blend of formal and informal activities. Virtual "lounges," or conference areas and chat rooms, are one way to obtain this mix. I incorporate informal spaces into all online conferences for which I have responsibility, although it takes a while before participants make good use of them. Early in my course, Shelly, an elementary teacher, commented on what she perceived to be a lack of casual conversation in the online forum:

> My communication with fellow students is extremely different online versus in person. As I was lying in bed last night I was thinking that every time I have ever taken a course, I have made a friend. This is usually done as we chitchat before the professor comes or at coffee breaks. There is not a place for this in an online course, I don't think. Perhaps in the lounge, but no one seems to be chatting there. I think that [the lounge] is where I will send this message.

After you fully adjust to learning in virtual communities, you may never find traditional learning and professional development quite the same. As Virginia said, "slow as it can be [to make change] and despite every obstacle, the kind of ripple effect that these new ideas and methods has is virtually unstoppable."

What Do I Need to Know to Join a Virtual Professional Community?

The Internet offers several technologies for accessing and building virtual professional communities. They are:

- Electronic mailing lists
- Internet newsgroups
- Proprietary conferencing systems
- Web-based conferencing systems
- Internet Relay Chat and MUDs
- Real-time Video Conferencing

In the next three chapters, I will describe each of these technologies, what they have to offer, and how you can make the best use of them. I will concentrate on the first two technologies, however, as they are the most widely used and offer the best choice of communities that you can join.

6 | Community Mailing Lists

Mailing lists are an excellent and exciting way to join a virtual professional community. They require only an Internet connection, e-mail software, and a valid e-mail address, together with some basic skills in knowing how to use them, which I'll cover in this chapter.

I'll start by describing what mailing lists are and how to identify lists that could be of interest to you. Then I'll deal with the mechanics of how to join lists, make use of their features, and contribute to them. Finally, I'll describe how you can be a welcomed addition to a mailing list community by contributing responsibly and sensitively to its discussions.

What Are Mailing Lists?

Mailing lists in their essential form are lists of electronic-mail addresses of individuals. After you subscribe to a list, when you want to communicate with members on the list, you send an e-mail message to a computer that automatically distributes your message to all names on the list. Similarly, when others send a message to the list, you automatically receive a copy of that message.

Tens of thousands of lists are maintained worldwide on computers connected to the Internet. Lists vary in size and frequency of use, from only a handful of subscribers who communicate infrequently, to thousands of members, many of whom contribute daily. Mailing lists are managed by special software on the host computer, called LISTSERV, Listproc, or Majordomo. You subscribe to a list by sending e-mail commands to the particular computer that manages the list you're interested in. There are some minor, yet important, variations in the commands you send to the mail server to subscribe and to perform other operations, that depend upon the mail list software. Lists can be public—they'll accept anyone who wants to join—or private—they are available only to a closed group of individuals such as employees of an institution, members of an organization, or a team of researchers. Most of the time when you join a public list, the host computer responds immediately by welcoming you to the list with a statement of its purpose and new-user information. Other times your subscription request has to be approved by a person who manages the list, which could take several days. If it's a private list, your request to join it may be politely refused.

So far I've described mailing lists in relatively mechanical terms. Mailing lists, however, are really communities of individuals, all sharing common interests, goals, ideas, or values. For the most part, members care enough about these common ties to be on a list devoted to maintaining them; to listen to what others have to say; and to contribute their own thoughts. Joining these communities can be both professionally and personally rewarding, because through active participation, you can get to know regular contributors well. You may even find that you develop direct, one-to-one e-mail relationships outside of the list on matters that concern you individually.

Identifying Interesting Lists

As you'll come to see later in this book in the section on research, the question you face with the Internet is usually not "Is there something that interests me?" but rather "How do I find what interests me?" Mailing lists are a case in point. There are lists ranging from the esoteric to the mundane, from the whimsical to the serious, and everything in between. For example, you can find lists on congressional debates affecting the arts and humanities (arts-all), issues affecting daycare providers (daycare-l), the use of crystals for healing (crystals), international discussions of students and faculty on ideas about k–12 school education (schooldays), polymer chemistry (polyed-l), fascinating and accurate trivia (factnews), and daily Jewish law (halacha-yomi) to name only a few.

As a starting point, I would certainly ask colleagues for names of lists they find valuable, monitor favorite professional publications' announcements of lists, and generally seek recommendations from those who are knowledgeable about professional resources on the Internet. Ultimately, these recommendations may save you some false starts and wasted time.

What Is Liszt?

There are some excellent tools to help you in your quest to find a community whose interests match yours. One tool you will almost certainly want to try is the Liszt Search-

Figure 6–1

Looking for an e-mail discussion group? Enter any word or phrase to search a *really big* directory of mailing lists-- 65,174 listserv, listproc, majordomo and independently managed lists from 513 sites (entire catalog updated on November 22, 1996):

able Directory of E-Mail Discussion Groups, popularly known simply as Liszt. To access this tool, point Netscape to *http://www.liszt.com*. You will then see a form into which you can enter keywords that describe your area of interest. Since the sample action plan given in the last chapter dealt with mathematics, I've illustrated Liszt by doing a search for groups available on this topic. I first entered the keyword "mathematics" into the search form, and then clicked on the *Search* button (see Figure 6–1).

After a few moments, Liszt returned a list of sixty-seven "hits." Each hit contains the name of the list and a phrase describing the list. Here's a sample of some of the hits:

List Name	Description
newinto-mathsed	Forum for student and new teachers of mathematics
south-western-math	Mathematics and NCTM Standards
TEACHMAT	Methods of Teaching Mathematics
TIMS-L	Teaching Integrated Mathematics and Science (TIMS) Project
atm-mail	Association of Teachers in Mathematics list
CPMP	Network of Chicago Public School Mathematics Teachers

mathed	Share ideas about computer issues in mathematics education
math-l	Mathematics Discussion Group
mlf-fract58	Mathematics Learning Forum—Fractions
uime	Discussion about using the Internet in mathematics education

List names are hypertext links to another page in Liszt. When you click on a name link, you see two items: (1) a link to a description of the list, provided by the list manager, and (2) a link to the commands you need to subscribe to and use the list. Liszt color codes the list names according to the amount of information on hand about the list, although in my experience this coding is not especially accurate. If Liszt doesn't provide a description of the list, you can obtain an "info" file for most lists via an e-mail request. When you click on the link to the list commands, you will find out how to request this file. The standard procedure is to send a one-word e-mail message (INFO) to the computer where the list resides.

When you begin a search with Liszt, you should initially choose a fairly general keyword or words. If that produces too many hits, start using more precise terms. For instance, if I had entered "elementary mathematics" and "teaching mathematics," both would have produced few hits. A word of caution, however: don't expect to do a sophisticated search, because the description of the lists in Liszt's searchable database is limited to short phrases.

Liszt is one of the most comprehensive databases of mailing lists, therefore it's an excellent tool to search for lists that match your interests and professional goals. I did a search on the following keywords (and variants of the words). Next to each is the number of hits Liszt produced.

Education	863
Teaching	451
School	461
Learning	238
K–12	35

While there is definitely some overlap in the lists (e.g., a list dealing with k–12 probably has an education focus), the number of hits listed above gives an indication of the number of lists that may be of relevance to teachers.

Another caveat is that a list's description does not always accurately portray the list's actual discussions. This is not the fault of Liszt; it uses descriptions provided by list managers. What sometimes happens is that a list is set up with a particular topic in mind, but over time members' interests shift and nobody bothers to update the list's description. The only way to be sure that a list meets your needs is to subscribe to it and read its postings, a process I'll describe shortly.

Other List Identification Tools

Liszt is one of the most comprehensive tools for mailing-list identification, but you are always wise in trying another tool if it doesn't help you find what you're looking for. The best single source to identify other tools is Yahoo! (*http://www.yahoo.com*). In the next section I describe Yahoo! in detail, so you may wish to familiarize yourself with that discussion before using the tool. Yahoo! is very easy to use, however. To locate links to dozens of other mailing-list search tools and guides, go to the Yahoo! main menu and click on the link to *Computers and Internet*, followed by *Internet*, and then *Mailing lists*. At that point, click on any of the links that appear interesting to you.

How to Join a Mailing List

To join a mailing list, you send an e-mail message to the computer that controls the list. The e-mail address that you use is the list's *administrative address*. This is the address that handles such operations as subscribing, unsubscribing, and receiving information about the list. Once you're subscribed, you submit messages for others to read to the *list address*. Everything sent to this address is distributed to all members of the list. It's essential that you understand that each list utilizes these two separate addresses. In addition, some lists publicize the address of the person who maintains the list. This is known as the list *owner's address*.

To illustrate the process of joining a list, I'll use the example of one list to which I subscribe, called WWWEDU. Your search of Liszt has informed you that this list's administrative address is:

> *listproc@ready.cpb.org*

and that the command for subscribing is:

> subscribe wwwedu Firstname Lastname

To join, you send an e-mail message to the administrative address, putting the subscription command on the first line in the message area. Substitute your first and last names for Firstname and Lastname. The command and list name are not case sensitive, but you should capitalize your name properly. Leave the subject line of your message blank. Do not put anything in the body of the message other than the subscription command, not even your signature. (Note that when you send a message to the administrative address of a mailing list, you should always leave the subject and signature out of your message.)

Shortly after you send the subscription message, you will receive an automated reply from the list containing further information about the list and, often, a welcoming statement from the list administrator. If you don't get an immediate reply, your subscription may require approval by the list owner. Here's an excerpt of what the list WWWEDU sends:

Dear user,

your request

SUBSCRIBE WWWEDU Ron Owston

has been successfully processed.

Welcome to list WWWEDU (wwwedu@ready.cpb.org). The system has recorded your address as

rowston@EDU.YorkU.CA

and it is required that you send your postings from that address, unless the list does not require subscription for posting.

The list's owners are acarvin@kudzu.cnidr.org.

You should contact them if there are any problems.

Please do not send requests to this list; instead direct them to:

listproc@ready.cpb.org

.

.

.

To get more information on how to use this service, please send the command HELP in a line by itself in a mail message to listproc@ready.cpb.org.

To signoff from the list, email to listproc@ready.cpb.org with the following request:

signoff WWWEDU

or

unsubscribe WWWEDU

*** WWWEDU—The Role of the World-Wide Web in Education

Hello, and welcome to WWWEDU!

First of all, I would like to thank you for joining WWWEDU—active since December 1994, it is now subscribed to by over 1600 people from 35 countries. As an informal, public discussion, WWWEDU can be a forum for all things related to the Web and education.

Never delete this message! Save it in a place you can easily access, because it contains helpful information about imporant list commands; even more important is that the message tells you how to unsubscribe from the list. WWWEDU requires that you put the command "unsubscribe WWWEDU" in the body of an e-mail message to *listproc@ready.cpb.org* to remove your name from the list. Not knowing this command could cause you lots of grief, because as a member of a list you no longer want to belong to, your incoming mailbox can get swamped very quickly with unwanted mail.

From the above excerpt, you can see that the list address is *wwwedu@ready.cpb.org*. Messages for distribution to list members are sent to this address. It could happen that when you post a message, it doesn't appear immediately. The reason for this delay may be that the list moderator has to approve your message before it is circulated. From the excerpt, you will also see that the list owner's address is *acarvin@kudzu.cnidr.org*. If you have any questions about the list that you do not want the entire community to see, you should direct them to this person. For general information about list commands, don't bother the administrator. Instead, simply send the word HELP in the body of an e-mail message directed to the administrative address. A list of commands and other information about using the list will then promptly be returned to you.

A convenient feature of WWWEDU that is not indicated in the excerpt but found in many other lists is the possibility of receiving list mailings in "digest" form. A digest contains the complete text of a day or more of postings to the mailing list. This is especially helpful for large, active lists because you sometimes get flooded with e-mail messages and it's difficult to keep list messages sorted out from other, perhaps more important, messages. The command to receive messages in digest form from WWWEDU is

set wwwedu mail digest

One final matter that you should be aware of is that lists normally require you to conduct all list business from the same e-mail address that you used to subscribe. You will recall that in the subscription command you did not specify your e-mail address. That is because the mailing list automatically gets your address from the header information that accompanies your subscription message. In practice, this means that you always have to use the same e-mail account to post messages or issue any other commands, including unsubscribing. For most people this should not create a problem; however, if your home e-mail address is different from your work address, you'll need to decide which address you would like to use for any particular mailing list.

On Becoming a Good Community Member

I have emphasized throughout that mailing lists are really communities of people sharing the same interests. As with any community, you must be sensitive to its established norms and practices to be welcomed when you join it. Think of what it's like to join a new club, organization, or faculty of a new school. Joining a mailing list is much the same. Generally speaking, all of the good practices of e-mail use discussed earlier apply when you post to mailing lists, such as including a subject and signature and using appropriate language.

To become a welcomed member of a mailing list community, there are several other practices you should observe.

- *Use Addresses Correctly.* Always make sure to send all commands to the administrative address of the list; postings go to the list address; and questions not covered by the list's help information can go to the list owner's address. If you mistakenly send commands to the list or owner's address, you'll likely be politely reminded by someone that you have made a mistake. However, if you do it more than once, the reminder may not be so polite! Sending postings to the administrative address is not as serious because the host computer will simply send you an automated message that it doesn't understand your command.

- *Become Familiar with the List Before Posting.* After you have subscribed, spend some time studying the list before posting any messages to it. By doing this, you'll become familiar with the nature of postings, including the style of language, range of topics covered, and common practices. You may even find that the list is on a totally different topic than its name implies. For example, you may be surprised to learn that a list named Hurricanes deals with a football team rather than a tropical weather system. Don't be afraid to send a message to the list owner if you have any questions about what topics are appropriate.

- *Be Mindful of Recipients.* As you'll recall from the discussion about e-mail, I said that you should never send an e-mail message to someone unless you would be comfortable seeing its content repeated on the evening news. This applies even more so to mailing lists, because your message will be broadcast to all list members, any one of whom may forward it to someone else. Therefore, messages should never be insulting, disrespectful, excessively personal, or abusive.

- *Consider Whether to Respond Individually.* Members often post questions or seek advice from others on the list. If you are able to respond, don't always assume your answer should go to the entire list. Sometimes it's more appropriate to respond directly to the individual who posed the question. You should ask yourself before sending to the entire list whether your answer is of general interest to all members. Some lists default to reply only to the sender; in this case, if you want your answer to go to the list you need to forward it or CC it to the list address.

- *Be Brief.* Keep your messages to the list as brief and to the point as possible. Mailing list servers become swamped if there is an excess of long-winded postings.

Limitations of Mailing Lists

I began this chapter by saying that mailing lists are an excellent way to join virtual professional communities. Their members tend to have focused interests and are helpful and committed individuals. Mailing lists, however, have drawbacks that you should be aware of too. One I've already mentioned is the possibility of having your In box easily overloaded. I personally find it oppressive to open my e-mail only to discover dozens of messages waiting to be read from only the day before. Therefore, I'm very judicious in my subscriptions and choose to receive mail in digest form, where possible. Check the Help file of any list to which you subscribe to see if digests are available.

Another limitation, particularly with large lists, is that it's sometimes difficult to follow the subject thread of a conversation. There are often so many different discussions taking place simultaneously that you may have difficulty tracking what is being said on a given topic. Newsgroup and special conferencing software typically have a feature that will allow you to read messages by subject; however, for mailing lists you are dependent upon whether or not your e-mail software has this feature.

A third shortcoming of mailing lists is that members don't always heed advice about proper use. Therefore, you find yourself wasting time reading messages from members asking questions such as "How do you sign off a list?" or "Are there digests of the list available?" And you'll also see postings that contain messages such as "I agree with what you said" without any reference to the statement that the person is responding to. Situations like this would not occur if all list users made proper use of quoting.

In conclusion, if you follow the advice given in this chapter and choose your lists carefully, you'll find that joining and participating in mailing lists can be a professionally rewarding activity. I'm sure you'll agree that their advantages far outweigh their drawbacks.

7 | Newsgroups

In this chapter, I will describe another way of building virtual professional communities—by participating in Internet newsgroups. Newsgroups are often described as the Internet's version of electronic bulletin boards, because once you post a message to a newsgroup, all visitors to that group can read and respond to it. Articles from some twenty thousand newsgroups are stored on servers connected to the Internet. Topics of these groups reflect the diversity of human interest, although educational, computer, and technical topics tend to be most heavily represented. Newsgroups offer an exceedingly rich opportunity to meet individuals worldwide with similar interests, to tap into their expertise and experience and to share yours, and to debate and discuss matters that you care about.

I'll begin the discussion of newsgroups by explaining exactly what they are and how they are organized. From there, I'll delve into how to read and respond to newsgroup messages. I'll conclude with an overview of how to use newsgroups appropriately and a brief discussion of their limitations.

What Are Newsgroups?

You'll hear newsgroups referred to as Internet newsgroups, Net news, Usenet news, or simply Usenet. I prefer calling them newsgroups and will do so throughout this book; however, Usenet is the technically correct name. The reason I prefer the term *news-*

groups is because the name *Usenet* conjures up different meanings to different people and is commonly misunderstood. Regardless of what name people use for them, they are all talking about the same entity: a discussion forum distributed worldwide.

You saw in the last chapter that with Internet mailing lists, list members receive copies of all list postings. Through subscribing once, you become a member of the mailing list community and continue to be a member until you unsubscribe. Newsgroups, on the other hand, operate on a different principle. All messages reside on news servers. When you want to see a newsgroup's postings or post a message yourself, you have to take the initiative to access the newsgroup rather than waiting for messages to come to you.

Newsgroups are distributed over many different networks, the Internet being just one. Like the Internet itself, there is no central authority or body controlling newsgroups. Not all newsgroups are carried by all news servers; it's up to the server administrator to decide what groups are to be carried. Nevertheless, there is a core of groups considered to be of sufficient interest to the Internet community at large that they are carried by almost all servers worldwide. Beyond these core groups, there are several other groups of more limited appeal that are commonly carried by most servers. In addition, servers usually carry newsgroups specific to their geographical area and groups set up by local organizations.

How Are Newsgroups Organized?

Newsgroups are organized hierarchically, much like the table of contents of a book. Most groups have subgroups, which are themselves often subdivided. For example, the group *news* is divided into thirty-seven subgroups (at the time of writing) ranging alphabetically from *news.admin* to *news.test*. Slightly fewer than half of these subgroups are further subdivided. The group *news.announce*, for instance, is subdivided into five groups, one of which is *news.announce.newusers*. As you can see, the group hierarchy is reflected by a period (.) placed between names, beginning with the top-level group. This provides a convenient way of locating groups on your news server. You know, for instance, that to find the group *news.announce.newusers*, you would first have to locate the parent group *news*, then the group *announce*, and finally the group *newusers*.

The top-level core groups carried by most news servers in the world are:

comp computer science and related topics of interest to professionals and hobbyists

msc a catchall group for anything that doesn't readily fit in elsewhere

news network news issues and discussions (but not current events)

soc discussion about social and political issues

sci both natural science and social science discussions

rec	arts, hobbies, and recreational activities discussions
talk	a forum for debates about controversial issues (e.g., religion, abortion)

In addition to these seven core groups, the groups usually carried by most servers include:

alt	often bizarre and notorious groups that discuss alternative ways of looking at things
bionet	biology-related discussions
biz	business discussions and the only group where commercial advertisements are acceptable
bitnet	many of the popular mailing lists are posted here
k12	student-teacher discussions

Other groups carried by a server depend upon its country, region, and city of origin. The news server I use, for example, carries groups from my own university (i.e., *york*) as well as other universities in the region, city of Toronto newsgroups (i.e., *tor*), and groups of interest to Canadians (i.e., *can*). Unless you received news from this same server, you would not likely have access to these groups, nor would I be able to access all of the groups carried by your server.

What If My News Server Doesn't Carry the Group I Want?

A problem arises when a group you want access to is not carried by your news server. In my case, two groups important to my work, *k12* and *schl*, both related to discussions about kindergarten-to-grade-12 education, are not carried by the server I use. If you find yourself in this situation, you have three options:

• *Contact the administrator of your news server or your Internet service provider.* If you have a persuasive enough argument, there's a chance your server will pick up the group or groups you are interested in.

• *Look for public-access servers that carry the group.* Most news servers restrict access to those groups that are in the same domain as the server. Some servers do allow public access, however. To locate these servers, go to Yahoo! and follow the path from its home page: *News and Media: Usenet: Public Access Usenet Sites.* Here you'll find a dozen or so links to listings of this kind of server, but be warned that these lists go out of date very quickly, so you may have to try quite a few servers before you are successful.

• *Try DejaNews.* I'll describe this excellent Web service in the section on conducting Internet research. Although intended primarily as a search service to identify newsgroups and topics of interest, you can read and post to almost any public newsgroup with DejaNews.

How Do I Access Newsgroups?

You can use specially designed newsgroup client software or Netscape to access newsgroups. This software is called a *newsreader*. It's the newsreader's task to sort out and present the newsgroups to you. Even though Netscape does not have as well-regarded a newsreader as some of the specialized clients, for simplicity's sake, I'll limit my discussion of newsreaders to Netscape. The chief differences between Netscape and the other better newsreaders lies in the latter's convenience of use and features. No matter what tool you use, you will always be able to access all groups carried by your news server.

Getting Started

Once you are connected to the Internet and have Netscape launched, you can read news by going to the *Window* pull-down menu and choosing *Netscape News*. (This choice is slightly confusing, because it erroneously implies that you are going to read news about Netscape.) You will then see a new window divided into three panes. You should see the name of your news server in the top-left windowpane. If this area is blank, it means that you are not connected to a server. Go to the *Options* pull-down menu, select *Mail and News Preferences*, and click on the *Server* tab. In the space for News (NNTP) Server, enter your server's address. Contact your network administrator or Internet service provider to obtain this address if you don't know it.

Click on the small triangle to the left of the icon marking your "default news host" in the left pane, go to the *Options* pull-down menu, and select *Show All Newsgroups*. You will then see a listing of the groups available on your server. The listing should look something like Figure 7–1.

Groups that have an asterisk (*) beside them are subdivided; the number of subgroups is shown in parentheses. When you click on the triangle in front of these entries, you will be shown the groups' subgroups.

The top-right windowpane of the Netscape News window shows the subjects of articles in any group you select; the bottom pane displays the contents of the message for any article subject you select. The screen shot in Figure 7–2 shows the selection of the group *news.announce.newusers*. This group is available on nearly all news servers. I recommend that you access it first to find out more about the correct use of newsgroups. A scrolling list of subjects appears in the right window, and once *Advertising on Usenet* is selected, the article's content appears in the bottom scrolling pane.

That is all there is to reading new articles. In summary, the basic procedure is:

1. Select a group in the left pane
2. Select a subject in the right pane
3. Read the content of the article in the bottom pane

Figure 7–1

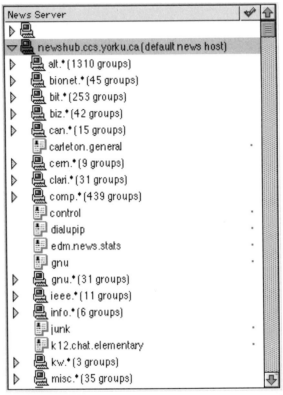

News Server

▽ 🖳
▽ 🖳 newshub.ccs.yorku.ca (default news host)
▷ 🖳 alt.* (1310 groups)
▷ 🖳 bionet.* (45 groups)
▷ 🖳 bit.* (253 groups)
▷ 🖳 biz.* (42 groups)
▷ 🖳 can.* (15 groups)
    📰 carleton.general
▷ 🖳 cem.* (9 groups)
▷ 🖳 clari.* (31 groups)
▷ 🖳 comp.* (439 groups)
    📰 control
    📰 dialupip
    📰 edm.news.stats
    📰 gnu
▷ 🖳 gnu.* (31 groups)
▷ 🖳 ieee.* (11 groups)
▷ 🖳 info.* (6 groups)
    📰 junk
    📰 k12.chat.elementary
▷ 🖳 kw.* (3 groups)
▷ 🖳 misc.* (35 groups)

You can alter the arrangement of the panes to suit your tastes in the *Mail and News Preferences* panel found under Netscape's *Options* pull-down menu. What you see in the screen shot is the default setting.

Navigating Newsgroups

You can navigate up and down the list of articles by clicking on the *Previous* and *Next* arrows along the toolbar. After you read an article and move on to the next, notice that the typeface of the subject line changes from bold to plain. A boldface subject line indicates an unread article. Next time you return to the group, the articles you've read won't appear in the list. To view them you must go to the *Options* pull-down menu and select *Show All Messages*.

Figure 7–2

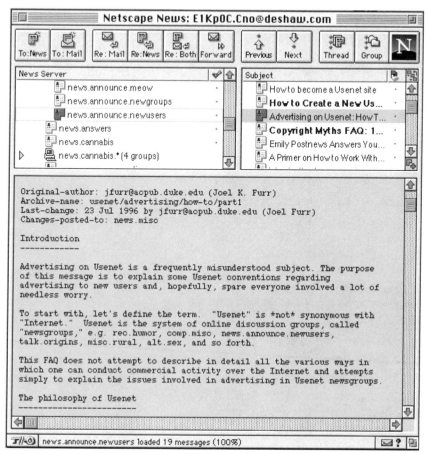

You can also mark an entire newsgroup or series of postings within a group as having been read by clicking on the *Group* or *Thread* buttons on the toolbar. This is a handy feature, because the next time you return to the group, you will see only the new postings for that group.

Subscribing to Newsgroups

When you first launched the Netscape newsreader and selected *Show All Newsgroups*, you probably noticed that it took some time for all of your server's newsgroups to appear in the window. You won't want Netscape to display the entire list of groups available each time you use the newsreader, because there are many groups that won't interest you in the slightest. To customize this list, you can "subscribe" to newsgroups that you regularly use. Then when you start up your newsreader, only these subscribed groups will appear in the left pane. To subscribe to any group, click to the right of its name and you'll see a check mark. Any time you want to see the groups to which you've subscribed, select *Show Subscribed Newsgroups* from the *Options* pull-down menu.

Posting and Responding

The most professionally rewarding aspect of newsgroups is the opportunity to actively participate in them by posting your own messages or responding to others. The process of posting and responding is very straightforward. First, select a newsgroup in the left pane if you are posting a new article, or select the article in the right pane to which you are replying. Next click on the appropriate button from the toolbar across the top of the News window. From left to right, your button choices and their purpose are:

To: News. To create and post an original message to a newsgroup.

To: Mail. To send an original e-mail message to someone.

Re: Mail. To reply directly to a person who posted an article. Frequently, it's more appropriate to reply to an individual than to the entire group.

Re: News. To reply to an article. The reply will go to the entire group and usually will appear as a new article within a day or so.

Re: Both. To reply to both the person who initiated an article and to the whole group. This option provides some assurance that if an article originator misses your reply in the newsgroup, they'll get it in their regular e-mail.

Forward. To forward an article in a newsgroup to someone else, or possibly to yourself for future reference.

Once you make your selection the Netscape Mail window appears. If you are posting a new article, the name of the newsgroup automatically appears in the address field. If you are replying to a message, the name of the newsgroup or the address of the article's author and the subject of the message appear in the proper fields. Enter your message and then click on the *SendNow* button to have the message delivered.

Appropriate Use of Newsgroups

While newsgroup posting and replying is relatively easy to do, your use of these features should be guided by the norms of accepted practice by the entire newsgroup-using community and by the special practices followed within certain groups. These norms and practices are not always obvious, so here are some suggestions about how to proceed.

- *Follow proper e-mail and mailing list practices.* All of the good practices I suggested for e-mail and mailing lists apply equally to newsgroups. I recommend you review these practices in Chapters 2 and 6 before posting or replying to any newsgroup.

- *Become familiar with the group before you participate.* Before you post or reply to messages in any group, you should spend time following the nature of the discussions that are held there. Look to see if the group has a Frequently Asked Questions (FAQ) article. Many groups do. If you can't find a group's FAQ article, check to see if it's posted in the special group *news.answers*. Careful study of this article will avoid your posting questions that have probably been asked and answered countless times before.

- *Check if the group is moderated.* As with mailing lists, some groups are supervised. This means that all postings first go to an administrator who must decide whether or not to post them. This information is usually found in the FAQ for the group.

- *Quote selectively.* While it's helpful for others to know exactly what's being responded to, quote only what's necessary. This is especially important for newsgroups, because debates can get quite lengthy and you don't want to force readers to reread the entire set of articles. Newcomers to the discussion can easily review original articles in their entirety.

- *Cross-post selectively.* When posting an original article, you may want several different groups to see it. You can include the names of all the groups that you want to post to in the *To* line of your article. This practice, called cross-posting, is acceptable, although you should limit your posting to no more than about a half dozen groups; otherwise group members will not think you are seriously interested in their group.

- *Be mindful of resources.* When you post an article to one of the core groups, it is automatically sent to tens of thousands of computers around the world. Even though you may have "free" access to newsgroups, universities and other nonprofit institutions that host news servers have to pay for the resources and interconnecting data lines that you use. Therefore, opt for posting to a local group if the matter you are writing about is only of local interest. Keep your articles brief and to the point, and only reply to the entire group if your reply is of interest to everyone, otherwise reply directly to an individual. Furthermore, if you don't see your article right away, don't simply repost it, because it can take twenty-four hours or longer for an article to appear in a group. These may seem like trivial matters, but given the tremendous volume of messages that flow over the system every day, everyone must do their part to conserve resources and prevent the system from becoming overloaded.

- *Do not advertise*. Public-service announcements and similar kinds of notices that may be of interest to the entire community are accepted in most groups. On no account should you advertise a product or service in a group. Designated groups exist for that purpose. One of these is the *biz* group, which is specifically devoted to business advertisements. Also, some local and regional groups are set up for the sole purpose of carrying classified ads. Again, be sure to check with these groups for guidelines about what is acceptable use before posting to them.

Newsgroup community members are self-regulating. If you violate accepted practices, you'll probably get a reminder from someone. But be warned that gross violations of "netiquette" may result in others flaming you. I don't mention this type of rebuke to discourage you from using newsgroups, as I believe they are an outstanding resource for professional development. My concern is that you may innocently violate accepted practice. So please take the above advice to heart before you begin participating in newsgroups. You will be a welcome member of the community if you adhere to established guidelines.

Limitations of Newsgroups

In using newsgroups for professional development, two limitations are evident. First, there is literally a profusion of interesting news; you could easily get consumed by the desire to read it all. Newsgroups can be addictive! Your action plan time allotment should be carefully adhered to when using them.

Secondly, because there are so many newsgroups, it's going to take you some time to identify ones that meet your interests and needs. Don't be discouraged by the seemingly large number of trivial, offensive, or bizarre groups that you'll no doubt encounter during the sifting process. There are many excellent, serious groups composed of dedicated, knowledgeable individuals. Try using the search tool DejaNews, described in the next section, to locate these groups. And of course, seek recommendations from colleagues and watch professional journals to find out about groups that people in your field find helpful.

8 | Other Kinds of Virtual Professional Communities

Among educators, mailing lists and newsgroups are clearly the most popular kinds of Internet virtual communities. Their major advantages are that they:

- are accessible by anyone, from anywhere in the world
- can be accessed with free software
- offer the possibility of sustained professional discourse

But mailing lists and newsgroups are not the only communities thriving on the Internet. In this chapter I will review three other kinds of communities that you can join. Although none of these are able to satisfy all three of the above criteria as fully as mailing lists and newsgroups do, they offer potentially rich opportunities for professional development. The three communities described below are:

- proprietary conferencing systems
- real-time text-based systems
- live video-based systems

Proprietary Conferencing Systems

Proprietary computer-conferencing systems have been around since the early days of time-sharing computers and were adapted for Internet access as soon as it became clear that the Net was the preferred way to access them. They are called "proprietary" because they use software that is licensed and sold commercially by one producer who holds the rights to the software design. Conferences based on proprietary systems are normally closed to the public, as they are owned by and operated for a select group of users who have access IDs and passwords. Some users prefer proprietary conferencing systems to open public systems because of their unique design and controlled access. Many such systems exist. The one that I will describe, FirstClass, is perhaps the leading proprietary system. It incorporates features found in almost all others.

FirstClass Conferencing

FirstClass, sold by SoftArc, Inc. (*http://www.softarc.com*), is widely used by school districts across the continent and worldwide for professional collaboration and discussion. This system got a foothold in many school districts originally as a Macintosh-based local area dial-up bulletin board and e-mail system. From these roots, FirstClass has evolved into a full-fledged, Internet-accessible conferencing system for Macintosh and Windows computers. Besides being easy to use, FirstClass has an attractive user feature—all of its functions are centralized in one window called the Desktop. Figure 8–1 shows the Desktop of the FirstClass system that I use.

The Desktop feature conveniently locates e-mail and group discussions, which constitute the bulk of most people's online work, in one spot. E-mail and conferences are represented as folders on the Desktop, which makes participation in virtual communities that much easier, since conferences are only a few mouse clicks away! To read

Figure 8–1

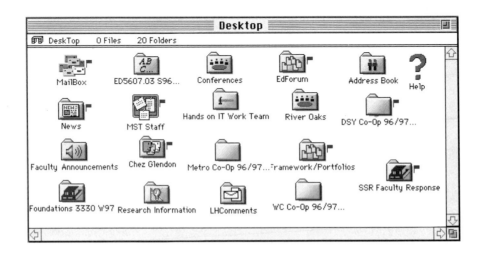

e-mail I double click on the top-left icon marked MailBox. I then see the screen shown in Figure 8–2.

Here I have private mail, including mail I received from mailing lists. To the left of the mail address is a flag indicating unread mail. The first three items also have icons beside them indicating that a file is attached. Across the top are folders that I created to file my mail.

Conferences are treated no differently from e-mail. For example, when I double click on the Desktop icon named EdForum, a group of folders appears, all of which are subconferences of EdForum. Each of these folders contains a list of participant contributions similar to my MailBox list.

Since more and more FirstClass systems are now linked to the Internet, conference participation is not limited to those in your own building or district. Many organizations use the system for Internet conferencing. My university, for instance, hosts several national and international conferences that bring together faculty, student teachers, and administrators to discuss and reflect on issues related to professional practice. One of the most established of these conferences, Writers in Electronic Residence, or WIER (*http://www.edu.yorku.ca/wierhome*), brings classroom teachers and their students together with Canadian professional authors to discuss one anothers' work. (Recall Marlene Bourdon-King's account at the beginning of Part III of how she grew professionally by being involved in WIER.)

Figure 8–2

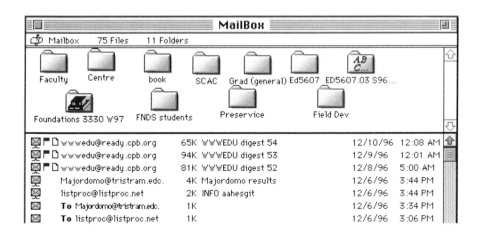

Real-Time Text-Based Systems

All of the virtual professional communities I have discussed so far—mailing lists, news-groups, and FirstClass—are called *asynchronous*, because people contribute to them at different times. Real-time or *synchronous* discussion is possible on the Internet too. Every day many thousands of real-time discussions take place on the Internet between two or more people on serious topics. People also gather simply to "chat" via the written word. The national newspaper *USA Today* has daily listings of real-time conferences that have broad public appeal, as does the Yahoo! Web site. These discussions frequently feature noted authorities in the arts, entertainment business, sciences, humanities, and politics. Other chat channels are dedicated to a wide range of special topics, including education. Be warned, however, that you will encounter many chat sessions that are trivial, sexually explicit, or offensive.

Real-time written dialogues have a somewhat limited appeal for professional-development purposes. One of the prerequisites for professional development via virtual communities is the ability to engage in sustained discussion. Real-time textual discussion is simply not a conducive environment to the fostering of in-depth exchanges over an extended period. Typing in text and waiting for others to respond is a very time-consuming process. It tends to encourage abbreviated, cryptic discussion. The reason I'm including real-time text systems in this book is because they do offer you the opportunity to engage in discussion people you ordinarily would not have occasion to talk to. For instance, if you are a science teacher, how often do you get a chance to ask a question of a Nobel Prize–winning scientist? With real-time systems, opportunities like this are possible. In addition, you can develop contacts for e-mail follow-up and get ideas and information from different sources.

Three systems are available for real-time text-based chatting:

- Internet Relay Chat
- Web-based chat systems
- MUDs and MOOs

Below I will give you an overview of each of these systems and point you to some useful references.

Internet Relay Chat (IRC)

IRC gained international prominence during the 1991 Persian Gulf War, and later in 1993 during the coup against Boris Yeltsin in the USSR. In both of these major world crises, IRC users gathered online to hear reports from eyewitnesses and to discuss the latest developments. Since then it has grown immensely in popularity and is constantly evolving technically. Essentially, IRC is an Internet-based system that allows people to communicate in group and private conversations in real time. To use IRC you need to have separate client software for your computer. With your client you connect to an IRC network via one of the network's servers. Once you are connected, you join a chat "channel" and carry on your conversation by entering your written text and by reading what others have to say.

There are many different IRC networks—three of the largest ones are EFnet (*http://www.irchelp.org*), The Undernet (*http://www.undernet.org*), and IRC-net (*http://www.funet.fi/~irc/*). If you point Netscape to the URLs for these networks, you will find their home pages, which contain information about the networks' general purpose, policies, operating procedures, and help files. You will also find a list of the servers that you can use to connect to the networks and descriptions of their chat channels.

If you are intrigued by the idea of carrying on live conversation with others around the globe with IRC, you first need to obtain the required client software. Several free and shareware (you pay a fee if you like the software) IRC clients are readily available on the Internet for Macintosh and Windows computers. The network home pages mentioned above have links to sites from which these clients can be downloaded. A popular Macintosh client is Ircle; mIRC is popular for Windows.

Once you connect to the Internet and start up your IRC software, you are ready to begin. Your client will likely come with a built-in list of network servers. Look for this list either in a separate window that appears when you start up or in a pull-down menu. Click on a network server that is close to you geographically, and enter your name or any pseudonym. (Use of pseudonyms is common practice on IRC.) If your client doesn't have a list of network servers, you will have to enter the server's URL yourself. You can obtain this information from the network's home page.

You are now connected to an IRC network. Next you need to join a chat channel. You will be able to obtain a list of all of the active channels, their subject, and the number of people currently using the channel by selecting the List command from a pull-down menu in your client. When you see a channel that interests you, click on the channel to join it. Usually you'll join in the midst of a discussion, so it's always wise to wait a few minutes to see what people are talking about before you begin to participate. Often one or two people will have noticed that you've joined from the participants list window found on most clients and will greet you. When you're ready to contribute to the conversation, enter your text into the appropriate window and press return.

After you become familiar with the basic operation of your IRC client, no doubt you will want to monitor Yahoo!'s home page to keep abreast of the latest IRC events. Click on the link to *Today's Web Events & Chats*. Here you'll find links to the day's and week's events as well to ongoing events. When you see IRC marked in the description of an interesting event, click on the link. The link will likely take you to the home page of the organization hosting the event. There you can get the name of the network, the address of a nearby server, and the channel name. Liszt, which was described in Chapter 6, also has a database of over 30,000 chat channels on 28 different networks that can be searched by keyword to help you locate IRC channels of interest.

Web-Based Chatting

If setting up and using an IRC sounds too complicated, you should know that you can also join real-time discussions via your own Web browser. Web-based chatting is growing in popularity because you can stay in the familiar environment of your browser and still access most of the features of IRC. Some sites require that you register, typically without a fee, before posting your own comments; however, almost all will let you view ongoing conversations without registering. Even though sites vary considerably in the actual mechanics of how you participate, no specialized knowledge is required.

As you visit Web sites for other purposes, you may encounter some that have Web-based discussion forums. Yahoo!'s *Today's Web Events & Chats* link is one source you will definitely want to check out. Again, be forewarned that you may encounter offensive language at some sites.

MUDs

MUDs—Multi-User Dungeons—are virtual-world role-playing environments. The first MUD was an online adaptation of the popular Dungeons and Dragons game. From this beginning, MUDs developed into text-based real-time adventure games where participants assume fictional identities and enter into simulated worlds. Out of MUDs grew several derivatives, MOOs, MUCKs, MUSHs, and MUGs. All of these are essentially the same from the participants' point of view, in that they require users to enter into a virtual world and assume a character role.

MUDs are hailed by their advocates as a new kind of social environment and have been applied to serious educational purposes. Virtual conferences, complete with different "rooms" for conference presentations and lounges where people can relax, chat, and have "virtual drinks," can be held using this approach. MUDs have also been incorporated into university courses, used for virtual meetings, rented out as virtual office space, and employed as environments for professional collaboration and research.

As fascinating as they are, however, MUDs are not likely to play a central role in your professional development today. In the future, they may well have a key role in professional development as they continue to be applied to education in innovative ways and as technical features evolve. For example, efforts are under way to extend them from text-only virtual environments to three-dimensional multimedia worlds, where you'll be able to learn through interaction with others in a graphical environment. I'll talk more about these kinds of environments in the final section of this book. If you wish to pursue this topic further, I suggest you follow in Yahoo! the path *Recreation, Games, Internet Games, MUDs, MUSHs, MOOs, etc.*, for more information and links to obtain client software, and watch the newsgroup *rec.games.mud.announce* for announcements about the latest MUDs available.

Live Video Conferencing

Live video conferencing is growing in popularity as more users gain high-speed Internet connections and software is improved. Like MUDs, video conferencing has limited application to professional development, though this may well change over the next few years. The software that started it all is CU-SeeMe, developed at Cornell University (*http://cu-seeme.cornell.edu*). CU-SeeMe is public-domain client software for Macintosh and Windows. When you launch the software, you can connect with it to any other person on the Internet, provided they also have the software, and you know their Internet address. Obviously, this type of conferencing requires a video camera and microphone as well as appropriate video and audio inputs on your computer. Once you're connected you will be able to see and hear and be seen and heard by the person you're connected to.

Video conferencing sounds almost too good to be true. And unfortunately, there is a catch—you must have a high-speed Internet connection to sustain the sound and picture quality of such a system. A 28.8K bps modem connection is insufficient. You need a minimum of a 56K connection and preferably much higher. If you have this speed connection, try downloading the software from Cornell and using it.

On the CU-SeeMe home page you will also see links to sites that host live video broadcasts and to "reflector" sites that allow you to have a mini video conference with other users. Also, Yahoo!'s *Today's Web Events & Chats* has links to current events and news broadcasts for which you don't need a camera—the broadcast you are able to receive on your computer monitor is just like television.

Part IV

Doing Research on the Internet

The mention of the word *research* often conjures up images of the lonely scholar working countless hours in isolation in a library or lab. Kimberly Loftin, an experienced elementary teacher in Stockton, California, shatters this illusion in her account below.

Currently I'm teaching fifth grade on a year-round calendar in Stockton for Lodi Unified School District, in an area of mostly low-income housing where three-fourths of our students are on a free-lunch program. Although I have enjoyed using the computer in my classrooms for ten years now, and even majored in computer science, whenever a new technology appears I feel once again that I'm a beginner! The Internet is no exception.

My first research undertaking involved looking for resources that my students could use on their upcoming state projects; I wanted to be sure the resources would be, in fact, available when they began their own research. I used Yahoo!, looking under the government and travel sections. I also searched through several education Web sites and discussion groups to see if other teachers had any tips on how to do this type of project. It was marvelous to discover that so many other teachers were using the technology in this new and exciting way.

My initial effort spurred me on to attempt further research. For my thesis project at Sacramento State, where I am just finishing my master's degree in curriculum and development by way of distance learning, I've been trying to find studies on the benefits and limitations of using the Internet in the classroom. I found only one empirical study when I searched in my university's library, so I turned to the Internet. I searched through discussion groups, subscribed to mailing lists, went through state departments of education, the Federal Department of Education, several other countries' education ministries, research laboratories, school districts making advanced use of technology, and countless—I mean countless—educational Web sites. One of the most important by-products of all this searching has been feeling the excitement (yes, that's possible over the Internet) generated by colleagues who are moving in the same direction. I now feel that I am part of a community of learners who are caring enough to help each other out, open enough to share new ideas, and determined to keep advancing professionally for the sake of their students. You can't find that in too many other occupations! The Internet provides me with access to thinkers with knowledge far beyond mine, at the touch of a key. It also gives me access to documents which are not yet published and those that possibly never will be. I further enjoy the ability to receive feedback from experienced users.

As a result of my online activities, I have learned how to work with my fellow teachers in different ways. Usually teachers are kept in small rooms with thirty-odd students with no time or vehicle for sharing ideas. The Internet has opened up the world for me. I regularly converse with teachers from all over. And surprisingly enough, I've found that teachers in other countries have very similar problems and accomplishments. My teaching has now taken on a much more global flavor.

9 | Why Use the Internet for Your Research?

Much of your professional-development time will be devoted to research on topics related to your action plan. You may want to hunt down an obscure historical fact, look for background details on today's news headlines, find out the latest thinking on constructivist learning, or track down research on teaching autistic children. Regardless of your topic, the Internet is the best single place to undertake your research. I will go as far as to say that if what you're looking for is not found, indexed, abstracted, excerpted, or referenced on the Internet, it's probably not worth reading! Some will find this statement outrageous. If they don't agree with it now, however, they may in a short period of time. The number of pages on the Web doubles in size every four months. By year's end in 1997, according to *Internet World* magazine, there were a staggering 200 million pages. Assuming this growth rate continues, by the time you read this, the Web will likely have surpassed one billion pages!

The Internet is rapidly becoming the repository for all new information, supplanting traditional print publishing as the way to disseminate new knowledge. Efforts are under way to put into electronic form the venerable classics in literature and other great works of the past. Even new commercially printed books, such as this one, inevitably have excerpts on the Internet as a way of supplementing, advertising, and promoting them. Major newspapers and magazines are also making available all or part of their contents on the Internet. There is every indication that not only will this trend continue, it will intensify, making the Internet a veritable global storehouse of the collective wisdom of humankind.

What the Internet Has to Offer Now

While the transformation of the Internet into a global knowledge repository marches forward, there is every reason that you should use the Internet today for your research. Here are some of the reasons.

Rapid, Up-to-Date Information

One of the stiffest challenges facing educators—and all professionals—is to keep up-to-date with developments in their field. Experts estimate that half of what an undergraduate in a professional area of study learns in his or her freshman year is out of date by graduation time. Fortunately, the Internet will help you stay abreast of advancements in your field of expertise, whether it be school administration, counseling, elementary teaching, or high school teaching.

You have probably noticed that these days whenever a major government report is published, a major news story breaks, a new commercial product is announced, or a scientific breakthrough is reported, a World Wide Web address is given for people wishing to obtain more information on the subject. This is because almost all producers of information, whether they be governments, academics, the news media, businesses, industries, groups, or individuals, have come to realize that if they want to broadly disseminate their information at a reasonable cost, they must publish it on the Internet. The result is a treasure trove of information for anyone who has Internet access. Moreover, this information is very up-to-date; oftentimes it's released on the Internet at the same time it becomes news—when a news conference is held or an announcement is made. So you don't need to wait for the information to appear in print the following day, week, month, or quarter. It's there on the Internet for immediate access.

Once you start to use the Internet for your professional-development research, your task of keeping current with your professional field of interest immediately becomes significantly easier. Of course, it's up to you to verify that the information you access is fresh. Many times you'll run across Web sites that contain stale information. Fortunately, the better Web sites tell you when they were last updated and are constantly kept current. When we look at Internet search strategies in this section, I'll remind you to watch for this date.

Much Information Available at Little or No Cost

Most educators find themselves in the unenviable position of having little money available for professional development—either from school districts or personal sources. This situation is unlikely to improve as legislators continue to look for ways to trim education budgets. The Internet offers a cornucopia of professional-development resources you can access at no cost, more resources than a local professional-development library or school could ever afford to assemble. Thus a school's or school district's investment in providing Internet access to its teachers is an extremely cost-effective strategy to aid teacher professional-development. Even if you have to pay for your own Internet access through a service provider, the money spent is a wise investment.

Ultimately, someone has to pay for the production of good quality information. Schools, universities, and other public and nonprofit organizations and agencies tend to absorb the costs of providing their information on the Internet because they see dissemination as part of their mandate. One example is the popular report of the Congressional Office of Technology Assessment (OTA), *Teachers and Technology: Making the Connection*. It's available for free on the Web at *http://www.ota.gov*, while if you want a hard copy you have to order it for nineteen dollars. On the other hand, commercial information producers need to recoup their development and operating costs. Several strategies have emerged to pay for these costs, all of which offer reasonable compromises for cash-strapped educators:

• *Advertising other companies' products or services is now a common way to pay for commercial Web site costs.* Popular Web sites now command advertising prices that rival the traditional media. The developers of search tools that you'll see in this section were among the first to embrace this approach. The user benefits, as this innovation allows for access to the best general search tools available on the Internet at no cost. The approach is popular because it offers advertisers access to select consumers who are likely to want to buy their product or service. If you are bothered by these ads, all you need to do is go to the *Options* pull-down menu on Netscape and deselect *Auto Load Images*. Then ad pictures will appear only when you specifically double click on their icons, which remain in their place on the page. (This option is the Internet's equivalent to the mute button on a TV remote control.)

• *Promoting a company's own goods or services is another way to cover the cost of Web sites.* The company's hope is that if you like the material you see at their Web site, you'll be motivated to purchase their product. Newspaper, magazine, and book publishers were among the first to adopt this strategy. They may make available on the Web all or part of a publication at no cost. Occasionally, these companies may request that you register by providing your name and address. This information is then used to obtain profiles of who accesses their site, or in some cases, to develop advertising mailing lists.

• *Charging a subscription fee is yet another way for information providers to pay their costs.* Practically all such companies provide free limited-time trial offers in the hope that you'll sign up for their service. Thus the information is there for your perusal, but you are under no obligation to purchase anything. Again, you should be aware that if you register for a trial offer, your name may be placed on an advertising mailing list.

Convenience and Time-Savers

Another advantage of using the Internet for your professional-development research is the convenience it offers. The busy workweek of most educators leaves little time to spare for professional development. Naturally you'll want to make the best use of whatever time you do have available for this purpose. I've already talked about how the Internet is quickly becoming the definitive source of global information. Only a few years ago you had to physically go to a library or other building where information was stored in order to access it. Now you can bring this information to you from practically anywhere in the world with no more than a few mouse clicks. Clearly, the Internet has produced a complete reversal of the paradigm of information access, a turnaround that is greatly to your advantage.

Exclusivity

The relatively high cost of physically printing and distributing materials is spurring information providers to publish only on the Internet. When you add to this the rapidly increasing proportion of the population who have Internet access, there's a compelling case for providers to only publish their materials electronically. Publishers of academic journals, particularly in the sciences, were among the first to capitalize on the strengths of the Internet for publishing. Their audiences were largely relatively sophisticated Internet users who needed to keep pace with rapid research advancements. Thus the Internet provided journal publishers with an effective solution to spiraling production costs.

More and more researchers as well as public and commercial organizations are joining the trend to publish only on the Internet. As this tendency continues, you stand the risk of overlooking key information sources if you do not use the Internet for your professional-development research. A short time ago, people viewed the Internet as little more than a minor supplement to traditional research sources. Now it's an essential source for all research.

Difficulties in Using the Internet for Research

This discussion on why you should use the Internet for your professional-development research would not be complete without some caveats. Under the best of circumstances, to thoroughly research a topic in an ordinary library is not an easy task for the uninitiated. To thoroughly research a topic on the Internet may seem even more formidable at first because there is no librarian to call upon if you get stuck. Nevertheless, the more you familiarize yourself with the Internet and its search tools, the more astute you'll become in your online research skills.

The difficulty of conducting thorough research on the Internet stems from the lack of a common indexing scheme for Internet materials. Anyone can make any kind of information available in any format without regard to any kind of cataloging conventions. In fact, unlike with traditional libraries, no universally accepted cataloging standards even exist. As a result, no Internet search tool stands a chance of being truly effective in accurately identifying all of the pertinent material on a topic. You will see in the next few chapters that many different approaches have been developed to overcome the lack of a cataloging system. Some of the tools are more effective at identifying certain kinds of topics than others, which means that you will have to learn to use several tools in your research. This is not quite as onerous as it sounds, however. There are many similarities among the tools, but each has its own strengths, weaknesses, and peculiarities that you need to be aware of.

Another challenge is that frequently your Internet searches will result in either (a) no material at all being found on a search topic, or (b) far too much material retrieved. This "all or nothing" dilemma can be dealt with by following appropriate search strategies, which I'll suggest later in this section.

Finally, once you retrieve a workable list of resources and set out to read them, you will notice that their quality varies dramatically. This problem is inherent in the Internet, where there are no restrictions on publication. While the Internet provides an unprecedented opportunity for freedom of expression, the unsuspecting reader may be profoundly misled by the contents of materials found there. In the traditional print medium there is some—albeit at times minimal—assurance that what you read has at least passed through an editorial process. Moreover, the name and reputation of the author and publisher are usually clues to the quality of what you read. On the Internet, the editorial stage is often bypassed, and you'll see materials that contain absolutely no indication of who or what organization posted the material. Therefore, there's a need to be even more of a critical consumer of information than in the past. In the final section, when I discuss the burgeoning size of the Internet, I'll suggest some criteria to evaluate the merit of material your research uncovers. Ultimately, you'll have to rely on your own best judgment based on your background, experience, and knowledge of your field to assess the value of what you retrieve.

10

Finding Information on the Web

Most of your research is likely to focus on retrieving information from the World Wide Web. Even though the Web is only a subset of the Internet, it is where people are now primarily publishing and making resources available. So I'll begin with a discussion of how to find information on the Web. You should bear in mind, however, that you may need to look beyond the Web to thoroughly research a topic. Some Web search tools will allow you to search Internet newsgroups, FTP sites, and various kinds of databases; I'll deal with searching non-Web sources later in this section.

What Search Tools Are Available?

An Internet commentator once said, somewhat tongue-in-cheek, that next to the Web itself, the fastest growing item on the Internet is Web search tools! New tools emerge every month, and today's hottest tools may seem antiquated by next year. Search tools normally fall into one of two general categories: indexes and directories. If you think of the Web as a gigantic book, Web indexes perform the same function as a book's index, referencing names, technical terms, and concepts found therein. Web directories are analogous to a table of contents, which helps you locate major sections and subsections of a book.

Web indexes were the first tools to be developed to categorize information on the Web. When the Web was taking root in the early 1990s, computer scientists at universities wrote artificially intelligent programs designed to "crawl" through the Internet unattended, collecting resources from Web sites. These data were then sorted, indexed, and made into searchable databases. One early example of an index is WebCrawler (*http://webcrawler.com*), developed at the University of Washington and now owned by America Online Inc. A more recent example, and one that I'll illustrate in detail in this chapter, is Digital Equipment's AltaVista (*http://altavista.digital.com*). Indexes offer the most comprehensive compilation of Web documents. When you search them, they tend to return extensive lists of documents, and the task of sorting through these resources can be daunting.

On the other hand, Web directories, in their simplest form, are merely catalogs of links to other Web sites. They contain main subject headings and several levels of sub-headings. Some directories are so vast that they have tools to search their contents. Yahoo! (*http://www.yahoo.com*), which started off as two graduate students' list of favorite Web sites and is now a publicly traded company, is the best-known Web directory. A major distinction between directories and indexes is the way their content is compiled. Indexes cast a broad net and mechanistically capture all that meets their data-collection criteria. Directories tend to be more discriminating. Human editors normally sift through Web documents and list those that meet a site's selection criteria. Summaries and capsule assessments are sometimes added to documents listed in directories. Directories tend to produce the most relevant results when you are searching for a general topic, but they may not be as comprehensive as indexes, nor are they necessarily as up-to-date.

In discussions of Web searching, the term *search engine* is often used. Search engines are the computer programs that assemble a Web resource database and enable it to be searched. AltaVista, for example, is a search engine. The distinction between search engines and directories is muddy—Yahoo! uses a search engine to retrieve documents from its own database of Web documents. Therefore, people may loosely refer to Yahoo! and other directories as search engines. What's important to you is not so much what each search tool is called, but how its database is assembled. In other words, you need to know whether a given tool attempts to capture the largest number of documents possible for its database, or whether its documents are gathered selectively by an editorial staff. Armed with this knowledge, you will then be able to properly interpret the results of your search.

I'll start the discussion of Web search tools with a look at indexes. Indexes require you to develop some expertise in mastering their search language, if you want to research more than a name or simple technical term. One of the biggest problems you will face with search tools of this type is narrowing your search sufficiently to produce a manageable number of documents relevant to your topic. I'll describe in detail how to conduct a Web search with AltaVista, one of the better-known and respected tools.

AltaVista encompasses almost all of the features found in other Web indexes, so the principles you learn for its use will equally apply to others. Following the description of AltaVista, I'll provide brief reviews of the other popular indexes that you may want to consider using for your research.

Web Indexes
AltaVista (http://altavista.digital.com)

Digital Corporation's AltaVista appeared on the scene in late 1995 to showcase what Digital's powerful new line of servers could accomplish. It boasts of having one of the largest databases of Web documents and excels in search speed. AltaVista indexes all of the words on each page of the documents in its database. This is unlike other search tools that may index only the title or summary of Web pages. As a result, AltaVista is capable of turning up even the most obscure references in little-known Web sites. The price you pay for this feature is that you will spend more time looking through AltaVista's list of "hits" to find the exact document you want.

Initiating a Search   You will probably most often find yourself wanting to search for a specific topic related to your professional-development action plan. For example, if you're a math teacher, you might want to see how other teachers are introducing fractals into their curriculum; if you're an elementary teacher, you may want to find out more on Reading Recovery programs; or if you are a principal, you may be seeking more information on school-restructuring initiatives.

To illustrate an AltaVista search, I'll describe my own actions in researching the virtual professional communities section of this book. I wanted to find out how teachers were collaborating over the Internet and how it aided their professional development, so I turned to AltaVista to see what had been written on the topic. I began with the word *telecollaboration,* a technical term that's used to describe collaborative interaction via telecommunications networks. I pointed Netscape to AltaVista's home page, *http:// altavista.digital.com.* In the form provided on that page, I entered the keyword *telecollaboration* (see Figure 10–1).

After clicking with my mouse on the *Submit* button, I was returned the results shown in Figure 10–2. AltaVista told me that the word *telecollaboration* appeared 739 times on four hundred separate documents. This suggests that "telecollaboration" appears, on average, slightly less than twice in each document. Note that the numbers given here were obtained when I performed the search. You would undoubtedly get different numbers if you conducted the same search today, because of the dynamic nature of the Web.

Figure 10–1

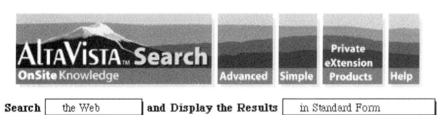

Search [the Web] **and Display the Results** [in Standard Form]

telecollaboration| [Submit]

Tip: To find how many external pages point to a site you're interested in,
try: **link:http://www.mysite.com -host:http://www.mysite.com**
The minus sign before a word means that the word MUST NOT appear in the document.

Figure 10–2

Search [the Web] **and Display the Results** [in Standard Form]

telecollaboration   [Submit]

Tip: To find a bed-time story: **"fairy tale" +frog -dragon**

Word count: telecollaboration:739

Documents 1-10 of about 400 matching the query, best matches first.

User Interface and Telecollaboration
> User Interface and Telecollaboration. User Interface and Telecollaboration. Need for a
> media-rich flexible user interface that can provide the information.
> *http://www.acl.lanl.gov/TeleMed/Papers/Object_World/tdt009.html - size 1K - 29 Apr 96*

User Interface and Telecollaboration
> Notes: 9.
> *http://www.acl.lanl.gov/TeleMed/Papers/Object_World/tdt009.html - size 1K - 3 May 96*

Telecollaboration Projects
> Telecollaboration Projects. GNN Education Center: The Great Match-Up. An online
> service which allows educators to both post ideas for telecollaboration...
> *http://teaparty.terc.edu/demo/resource/telecol.html - size 4K - 26 Jun 96*

Resources - Telecollaboration Projects
> Links to... Telecollaboration Projects. Knowledge Integration Environment A curriculum
> which allows students to integrate scientific evidence available...
> *http://teaparty.terc.edu/research/resources/tele-resr.html - size 6K - 13 Jun 96*

Ten document titles appeared on the first page AltaVista returned, although I've only shown four of them above. For each document, you see a few lines extracted from the document, its URL, and the document's size (in k) and the date that it was added to AltaVista. To view any document on the page, simply click on either its title or URL. To view the next page of documents, click on the page number at the bottom of AltaVista's home page. Occasionally you'll find the extracted text of a document unhelpful, so the only way to get an idea of what's in this kind of document is to view it.

Note that on the line indicating the number of documents found, you are told that the "best matches" appear "first." In other words, you are likely to find what you're looking for close to the top of the list. AltaVista determines what the best matches are by calculating a "relevancy score" for each document; however, unlike some of the other search tools, AltaVista does not tell you this score. The most "relevant" documents are those in which the search word is found

- in the first few words of the document
- in the title of the page
- more than once in the document
- in close proximity to other search words used, if any

Also note that, by default, AltaVista searches the Web. If you pull down the menu in the box next to the word *Search*, you can search newsgroups instead. In addition, you can display your search results in various formats, although the default standard form is probably the most useful.

A quick perusal of the documents I found showed that, even though those most relevant to telecollaboration appeared at the top of the list, many had nothing to do with teachers. Therefore, I had to come up with some strategies to narrow my search.

Narrowing the Search   To restrict the search to only documents that deal with telecollaboration and teachers, I entered the following:

+teachers +telecollaboration

AltaVista then returned a more manageable list of 125 documents. The "+" notation told AltaVista to retrieve documents that contain both the words *teacher* and *telecollaboration*. It doesn't matter which word appears first in the search string as long as both have a "+" in front.

After concluding this search, I realized that I may have excluded relevant documents by not incorporating forms of the word *teachers* such as "teacher" and "teaching." In this situation where you want to extend your search to forms of a root word,

AltaVista allows you to add the wild card notation "*" to the root. I resubmitted the search as

    +teacher* +telecollaboration

and found 142 documents, 17 that I would otherwise have missed.

When I looked through this new set of documents, I saw that some were dealing with the delivery of courses for teachers over the Internet, a topic that didn't interest me. To remove those from the list, I took advantage of the "−" notation, and entered

    +teacher* +telecollaboration −course*

which excluded all documents containing the word "course" or "courses." The result was 106 documents.

My list of of documents was now taking shape, but it was still fairly large, so I decided to see if any of the documents dealt specifically with professional development. To accomplish this, I added *professional development* to the search string and surrounded the words with double quotes (" "). The search terms now looked like this:

    +teacher* +telecollaboration -course* +"professional development"

The double quotes tell AltaVista to look for documents containing the words together, as a phrase. In general, you can ask AltaVista to search for any string of words by surrounding the string with quotes. After I clicked on *Search*, AltaVista returned nineteen documents matching my search criteria, all of which proved to be pertinent. Finally, I added the search terms to my set of Netscape bookmarks, a feature that not all search tools have. This allowed me the possibility of redoing the search at any time.

Searching for Names   Another type of search you'll frequently do is for people's names or other proper nouns. AltaVista makes a distinction between upper- and lower-case letters to aid you with this kind of search. The general rule is that if AltaVista sees a lower-case letter, it will find both upper- and lower-case instances of that letter; if it sees an upper-case letter, it will find only upper-case instances. In my research on virtual communities, I wanted to see what I could find on the well-known author and speaker Howard Rheingold. I entered the search terms

    "howard rheingold"

and as you can see, I used only lower-case letters. I did this because AltaVista will thereby search for HOWARD RHEINGOLD, Howard Rheingold, and all other variations of this name in upper- and lower-case letters. However, if I used standard capitalization in the search term (Howard Rheingold), AltaVista would not search for documents in which his name was spelled all in lower case. Since many Web documents are informally written and often not edited carefully, finding a name spelled all in lower case is not unusual. Therefore, I may have missed some important resources if I had entered it using the standard capitalization.

The case sensitivity of AltaVista is particularly useful when making a distinction in your search between, for example, apple, the fruit, versus Apple computer; or turkey, the fowl, versus Turkey the country.

In my search for Howard Rheingold, you'll notice that I surrounded his name with double quotes. Using the quotes yielded about three thousand hits; when I removed the quotes, eight thousand documents were retrieved. This is because, in the latter search, AltaVista retrieved documents containing only "Howard" or only "Rheingold," in addition to documents in which these names occurred together. The quotes forced AltaVista to find both Howard and Rheingold together as a phrase, which yielded a more meaningful result.

Advanced Searches   What I've shown so far will likely help you in 95 percent of your searches. Occasionally, you'll encounter difficulty finding the right kinds of documents using these simple query procedures. In that case, you may wish to try the advanced search features of AltaVista. To use these features, click on the icon marked *Advanced* on the AltaVista home page. You'll then see a new form for entering your search words and for indicating how you would like to have your results displayed. With this form, you are required to use binary, or Boolean, operators between your search words: AND, OR, NOT, NEAR. Though standard AltaVista searches make use of these binary operators in a less formal way, the Advanced Search page requires that you be explicit in their use. For example, when you enter

- cats AND dogs, documents containing *both* these words are returned
- cats OR dogs, documents containing *either* of these words are returned
- cats AND NOT dogs, documents containing the word *cat* are returned, provided they don't also have the word *dogs* in them (Note that in AltaVista NOT cannot stand alone—it must be used with AND.)
- cats NEAR dogs, documents containing these words in close proximity are returned

The Advanced Search page also allows you the option of specifying which documents are ranked first when the results are displayed. For instance, if you searched for "cats AND dogs," you could tell AltaVista to display documents with the word *cats* appearing first at the top of the list.

Excite (http://www.excite.com)

Excite not only has one of the larger databases of Web documents, it has a unique directory of over sixty-one thousand Web sites that professional journalists have reviewed and rated. About half of Usenet's newsgroups can be searched, as can newsgroup classified-advertisements. Excite's database is built using a "spider" that visits Web sites and extracts key concepts from pages. You can perform searches using the same notations as you use for AltaVista, except that you cannot use the Boolean "NEAR" operator. An added feature is the ability to increase the importance (or weighting) of any word in a search string. Search results are displayed with an indication, in percentage, of the confidence that an item matches your search criteria. The title of the document, its URL, and a summary of several lines is also given. Another convenience is the ability to refine your search by asking Excite to find more documents similar to any one that you retrieve. Excite's home page is relatively cluttered with hot links and advertisements. At the time of writing, the service consistently responded slower than most.

HotBot (http://www.hotbot.com)

Aimed solely at Web searching, HotBot is designed using technology whose capacity can be readily increased as the Web grows. HotBot's goal is to be the most comprehensive and up-to-date search tool available—a goal that is within its reach. Via a pull-down menu, HotBot offers a full range of search options. A valuable feature not found on other search engines is the option to limit your search by document date, media type (e.g., Acrobat, Shockwave, or specific file extension), and global location. HotBot's search results contain the document title, its URL, and a percentage relevancy score. Each result has a few lines of descriptive information on the document's contents, most of which is not especially enlightening. Performance is snappy and the home page is uncluttered and attractive.

Infoseek (http://www.infoseek.com)

Infoseek was designed with speed in mind, as well as expansion, as demand for its services and the size of the Web grows. I found validity in the speed claim; it consistently performed as fast as any of the search engines described in this chapter. Another claim made by Infoseek is that it handles queries stated in ordinary language (e.g., what is the capital of Canada?) better than other search engines and returns more relevant results. Among the unique features Infoseek offers to back up this claim is its ability to find words regardless of spacing between them (e.g., data base vs. database, key word vs. keyword). It even has the ability to find variants of words (e.g., a search for "mice" will include "mouse"). Your ability to control the search syntax recalls AltaVista, but Infoseek does lack several of the advanced features that its rival has to offer. Infoseek's home page is laid out clearly, without excessive distractions from advertisements. The search-results list yields the relevance of each document (in percentage) and a line or two describing the documents.

Lycos (http://www.lycos.com)

As one of the oldest and most comprehensive search tools, Lycos has long been considered the standard of comparison for new search services. Its database is built using a "spidering" technology that the company claims enhances the relevancy of search results, ensuring that returned documents contain your search terms as part of their central theme. You don't have the flexibility and control that AltaVista provides in specifying your search criteria, but there is an advanced search form that lets you choose whether the search terms are connected with AND or OR and indicate the strength of the association among the terms. A feature not found in other search engines is the ability to search for multimedia files on the basis of their description, rather than by their exact name and file type. Lycos has a subject listing of the most popular Web sites that can be browsed, as well as a listing of evaluated sites that are claimed to be the best 5 percent of the Web. Among the summary information found on retrieved documents is a relative ranking of the list of documents, the number of links to other Web pages contained in the document, the words matched on the document's page in Lycos's database, and an abstract.

Open Text (http://www.opentext.com)

Open Text contains a full-text database, though it is not as large as AltaVista's, Hot-Bot's, or Infoseek's. Using Web "crawler" technology, Open Text claims that some fifty thousand entries are either added or updated each day, although I have not found it to be as current as the other search engines described here. Search capabilities rival those of AltaVista. You have the option of searching with the default search form or a power search form that allows Boolean operations. There's a handy "graphics light" option for slow Web connections. Regardless of whether I used this option or the standard view, I found Open Text to be consistently slower and I received more "server busy" messages with it than with any of the other services discussed in this chapter. The results page is clearly and neatly laid out. It contains several sentences describing the retrieved documents; you can choose to see where the matches of your search words were found in the documents; and you can search for pages similar to any retrieved page. Although documents are ranked in order of relevance, the four-digit relevance score provided does not give you much sense of how closely a document matches your search words.

Webcrawler (http://webcrawler.com)

Webcrawler offers a modest-size, full-text database that performs snappily. It has a clean, straightforward home page layout. Underlying its uncomplicated appearance is a search engine that allows ordinary language queries, as well as more advanced searches.

The advanced search language rivals AltaVista's on most features and offers slightly more flexibility when searching for words located close to each other. Search results come with a two-to-three-line summary, a percentage relevancy score, and an option to find similar pages. Its chief drawback is that it is less comprehensive than any of the other search engines reviewed here.

Which Web Index Is Best for My Research?

One fact is clear when deciding which index to use for your research—you cannot take at face value the claims made by most sites that they are the fastest, have the largest database, or produce the most relevant search results! You'll probably find that no single tool will satisfy all of your research needs. If you're searching for popular Web sites or for well-known documents, any of the tools will efficiently locate what you're looking for. On the other hand, if you're trying to locate an obscure Web site, or if you want to make certain you've exhausted all possible recent occurrences of a search term, then my experience suggests you try HotBot.

Beyond these recommendations, the decision about which search engine to select for your research purposes is not clear-cut. If you have a fairly slow Internet connection, I suggest you avoid Excite and OpenText. If you require maximum control of how your search is conducted, AltaVista is probably your best bet. When you don't need a high level of control, you should try HotBot, because of its simple yet powerful interface, or Infoseek, because of its ability to handle ordinary language queries. None of the other tools reviewed seemed to provide the comprehensiveness, flexibility, and speed that AltaVista, HotBot, and Infoseek offer. In choosing among these three, you will no doubt be successful in your search.

Comparing Web Indexes Yourself

Now that you have some indication of the relative strengths of Web indexes, why not try a quick comparison of them yourself? Remember that by the time you read this, new indexes will undoubtedly be available and existing ones may be upgraded or neglected. Look for answers to these questions:

• *How up-to-date is the index?* Search all of the indexes for a Web site that you know has recently been created, be it devoted to a well-known person or an event that's currently in the news. It may even be the site of a new school or other organization that you know has recently been set up.

• *How relevant is its information?* Try searching on the name of several large well-known companies. All indexes will produce hits, but the better ones should produce the companies' home pages at the top of the list.

• *How does it handle a complex query?* Enter a complex phrase describing a topic you know well. The better indexes should produce a list of documents, containing the most pertinent one at the top.

Web Directories

There's a multitude of Web directories available—so many that you could easily spend all of your research time simply browsing them! My suggestion is to use only a few directories, ones that you feel comfortable with, that have the kind of content you generally need, and that are kept up-to-date. Yahoo! is definitely one that you'll want to keep returning to, as it is the most comprehensive and up-to-date directory of Web resources. I also recommend three other directories for professional-development research: Argus Clearinghouse, Magellan, and the WWW Virtual Library. As all four represent different approaches and philosophies to directory building, I will describe each in some detail.

Locating Key Resources with Yahoo!

Yahoo! represents an attempt at the Herculean task of organizing all Web resources into a convenient-to-use directory. Indeed, it has been compared to the work of the eighteenth-century botanist Linnaeus, who developed a classification system for the natural world. Yahoo! is most helpful when you want to quickly locate the key resources directly related to a general area of interest; but it is not particularly useful for finding obscure references to technical terms or persons' names.

When you point your browser to Yahoo!'s home page at

http://www.yahoo.com

you'll immediately see two columns of links to general categories, together with subcategory links. The subcategories will either link you directly to relevant Web sites or they'll contain further subcategories. Yahoo!—like all directories—does not contain much original material itself; it's essentially a directory of links.

To illustrate the difference between Yahoo! and AltaVista, I'll continue with my example of looking for resources on virtual communities. When I entered "telecollaboration" in the search box at the top of the Yahoo! page (see Figure 10–3) and clicked on *Search*, no references were found. This is not surprising, however, as Yahoo! does not have a subcategory on telecollaboration and its link descriptions are terse.

A better way to pursue the topic is to click on *Education* and see Yahoo!'s complete list of subcategories, ranging from Adult and Continuing Education to the Workplace (see Figure 10–4).

Figure 10–3

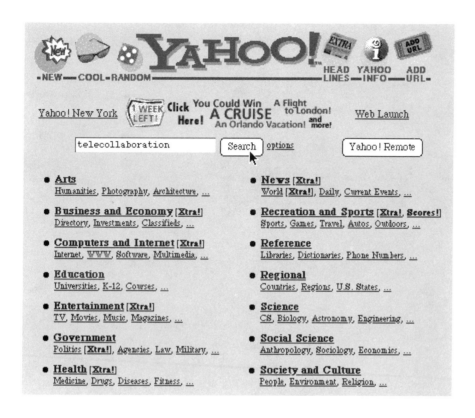

Several items on the page shown in Figure 10–4 should be noted. First, you'll notice that after most entries there's a number in parenthesis. This indicates the number of items found under each heading. You'll also see the "@" sign after the entries for *Companies* and *Interest Groups*. This tells you that the heading is listed in multiple places in Yahoo! When you click on it, you'll be taken to its primary location. At the top of the page you'll see two other links: *Sub Category Listing*, which shows all of the subcategories under each of the headings on the page, and *Indices*, a very handy feature which takes you to links to other relevant Web directories related to the topic of the page you're currently viewing.

The links *Teaching, K–12*, and *On-line Teaching and Learning* appeared relevant to the topic of telecollaboration, so I clicked on *Teaching*. A long list of links then appeared under this heading.

Figure 10–4

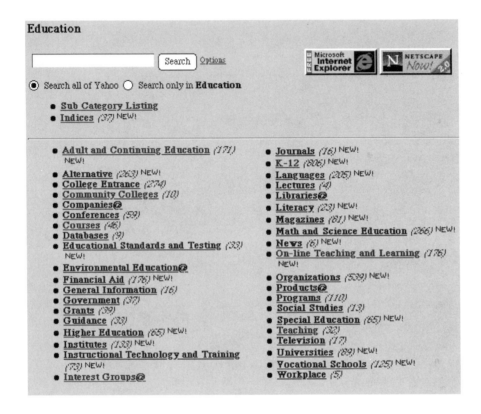

Since I didn't want to browse through each link description, I decided to do another search, this time using the search options feature. I clicked on *Options* and was taken to a form wherein I could fill in my search criteria. I decided to try the search words "talk," "support," and "collaborat." I chose to search on "collaborat" because Yahoo! will search for words with that as the root (e.g., collaborative, collaborating). You will see that I restricted the search to the Teaching category and asked for Yahoo! to retrieve links containing at least one of the three search words. I left all other items on the form in their default settings (see Figure 10–5).

After clicking on *Search*, Yahoo! found six links meeting my criteria, three of which I found relevant to my interests.

Overall, you'll find Yahoo! extremely convenient and easy to use. I recommend it if you are just starting to explore the Web. Tools like AltaVista can be intimidating

Figure 10–5

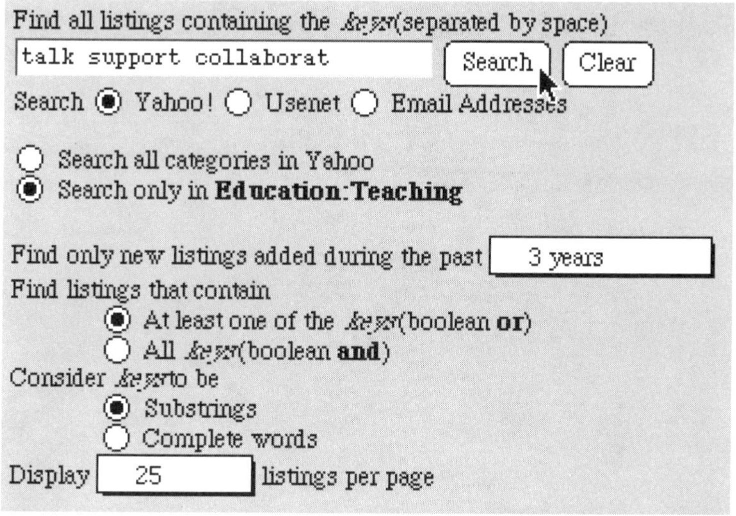

```
Find all listings containing the keys (separated by space)
talk support collaborat        [ Search ] [ Clear ]
Search  ● Yahoo!  ○ Usenet  ○ Email Addresses

    ○ Search all categories in Yahoo
    ● Search only in Education:Teaching

Find only new listings added during the past [ 3 years ]
Find listings that contain
        ● At least one of the keys (boolean or)
        ○ All keys (boolean and)
Consider keys to be
        ● Substrings
        ○ Complete words
Display [ 25 ]  listings per page
```

because of their nature and the sheer number of resources you retrieve with them. Yahoo! is expanding rapidly into the development of specialized directories for specific cities (e.g., New York, Los Angeles), countries (e.g., Canada, Japan), and segments of the population (e.g., Yahooligans! for children). Links to these directories can be found at the bottom of Yahoo!'s home page.

The Argus Clearinghouse: A Professionally Maintained Directory (http://www.clearinghouse.net)

Originally established as the *Clearinghouse for Subject-Oriented Internet Resource Guides* by librarians at the University of Michigan, the Argus Clearinghouse is now an independent organization. Beneath a dozen headings ranging from Arts and Entertainment to Social Sciences and Social Issues are over four hundred subject guides to Internet resources. What is unique about the Clearinghouse is that its guides are maintained by either a librarian, an educator, or another professional active in the field. The Clearinghouse requires that guide authors be identified and that guides conform to strict submission criteria. All new guides are rated on a five-point scale by Clearinghouse staff and provide the date of their last staff review. Guides vary considerably in when they were last reviewed, but generally staff place older guides under a separate page heading.

No two guides found at the Clearinghouse follow the same format; however, because of the submission standards, you have reasonable assurance that material in a guide is representative of the best resources available in a particular subject. Most resources found in the guides are Web-based, but you will also find references to newsgroups, Telnet, and FTP resources. All guides come in hypertext versions, though some come with a plain text version as well. There is a facility for carrying out simple Boolean searches (AND/OR) of guide title pages, which include author, institution, and keyword descriptors of its content. The full text of guides may be searched as well.

The Clearinghouse has an uncluttered and functional home page, free of advertisements. Browsing its directory is simple and problem free. In short, if you're looking for a directory that is more academically oriented than the typical commercial directory, the Clearinghouse is an excellent resource.

Browsing and Searching Evaluated Resources with Magellan (http://magellan.mckinley.com)

Magellan is a comprehensive directory of Web as well as Gopher, Telnet, FTP, and newsgroup resources. From its well-laid-out home page, you have the choice of immediately browsing Magellan's hierarchical subject directory, which has main topic headers ranging from Arts, Education, and Law, to Politics and Travel, or you can search its database. The database contains documents reviewed and rated by staff and a large collection of yet-to-be reviewed documents. Reviews provide sufficient detail for you to get a good idea of the content of documents without having to link to them. Magellan's rating system awards up to four stars based on depth of document content, ease of exploration, and net appeal (visual appeal, innovative use of Web technology). A unique feature—and one that we'll no doubt see more of soon—is that reviewed sites containing "no content intended for mature audiences" are given a green-light icon. The green light, naturally, applies only to the document itself, not to any of the sites you might access through links.

The search capabilities of Magellan are powerful, rivaling those of AltaVista and far exceeding Yahoo's. Not only can you search the main database, but you can restrict your search to reviewed sites and even to green-light sites. This is an extremely handy feature when trying to identify sites with which to begin your research on a specific topic. For example, I entered the term "+teacher +resources" (without the quotes) to identify sites for teacher resources. An unrestricted database search yielded some 38,000 sites, an unworkable number. However, when I restricted the search to reviewed sites, 128 were found. (Restricting the search even further to only green-light sites yielded 104, though its hard to imagine what the 24 teacher-resource sites without green lights would contain!) I finally restricted my search to reviewed sites that had been given a four-star rating; Magellan found 15 of them.

Accessing Global Resources via the WWW Virtual Library (http://www.w3.org)

The third directory I recommend for your research, the World Wide Web Virtual Library, has some features common to the Argus Clearinghouse, but is different enough from Argus to warrant your close examination. Tim Berners-Lee, creator of the World Wide Web, started the Virtual Library at CERN in 1991 to keep track of Web developments. As the library began to grow, the idea of distributing the responsibility for maintaining it to researchers around the world emerged. The library was eventually moved from CERN to its present location at the W3 Consortium, a nonprofit industry organization that seeks to promote standards for the evolution of the Web.

The Virtual Library consists of a large central directory providing links to scholarly documents, resources, and databases across the Internet. To access it, click on the link *Virtual Library* on W3's home page. When you select a topic heading from the Virtual Library's home page, you link to another Web site elsewhere in the world that provides access to resources on that topic. The resource sites are maintained by an academic institution, organization, or society, or by individual researchers. What's especially attractive is that the resource sites are scattered across the globe, so you are almost certain to get a different perspective on what documents and resources are key to a given field than you would from most of the other indexes and directories I've talked about. Another inviting feature in this day of rapid commercialization of the Web is that, by agreement, sites listed at the Virtual Library are prohibited from displaying advertisements.

You have the choice of several views of the subject headings on the Virtual Library's home page. The view you first see is an alphabetical list of some 150 subject headings. In addition to the traditional academic subject headings you'd expect (e.g., Anthropology, Chemistry, Physics), there are headings for specialized areas of research such as Drosophila (fruit fly), Migration and Ethnic Relations, Spirituality, and Vision Studies. When you click on the link *Category Subtree* at the top of the page, you see main subject headings followed by topic subheadings. This view may provide a more efficient way to browse the list of topics, because you can zero in on your area of interest more quickly. Clicking on the *Library of Congress Classification* link gives you a view of the directory list that conforms to LOC's standard headings. As with all good Web sites, the Virtual Library indicates new additions to the directory list; these are marked by a colored icon.

In short, you will want to visit the World Wide Web Virtual Library if you are searching for links to resources on academic topics that are noncommercial and maintained by institutions and specialists in the field.

Which Directory Should I Use?

The four directories reviewed here comprise a powerful arsenal of tools to research just about any topic related to your professional development. If you're beginning research on a new field of study, you may wish to start by looking at Magellan's three- and four-star rated sites (e.g., those on biology, mathematics, reading, and special education). From there, you might expand your search to Yahoo! You can rely on Yahoo! to be both comprehensive and up-to-date. Then you'll want to check both Argus Clearinghouse and the World Wide Web Virtual Library, especially if you are having trouble identifying relevant resources. Afterward you may also want to look at the subject directories found on several of the Web indexes I've reviewed, such as Excite, Lycos, and Infoseek. Even if your chosen field of study is not new to you, I suggest you check these three sites from time-to-time to watch for new resources.

Should I Use an Index or a Directory?

You'll recall that I began this chapter by describing Web indexes and directories as analogous to indexes and tables of contents of books. In the final chapter of this section I will give you suggestions for developing comprehensive research strategies. In the meantime, keep this analogy in mind and follow the rule of thumb: if you're looking for specific information on a topic, try an index; if you're looking for general information, try a directory.

11 | Searching Bibliographic Databases

Your browsing of education links in Web directories will eventually lead you to two kinds of bibliographic resources that should form part of your overall research strategy. One is the catalogs of holdings of major public and university libraries around the world. The other is the ERIC (Educational Resources Information Center) database of educational resources. The ERIC database is the most comprehensive index of published and unpublished articles, papers, books, and reports related to the general field of education that is available. These two sets of resources have at least three features in common that distinguish them from the resources I've talked about so far.

First, although the home pages of libraries and public-access ERIC sites can be located with your Web browser, they often require a Telnet or TN3270 connection for you to access them. This is changing rapidly, however, as more and more libraries and ERIC sites construct Web-based forms for searching their databases. In the meantime, having to use Telnet or TN3270 may seem like a nuisance, and their use may be intimidating for those unfamiliar with these tools. But when you set up your Web browser properly, the Telnet or TN3270 connection is made automatically from Netscape simply by clicking on a Web link. The only difficulty you'll encounter with these tools is that you are no longer able to use your mouse, because Telnet and TN3270 are not graphical tools, and some keyboard keys, such as backspace and delete, are disabled.

The second distinguishing feature of these databases is that, unlike documents published directly on the Web, library and ERIC resources are systematically cataloged and described by standard keywords. This feature greatly increases the likelihood of finding items that you want, or at least enables you to confidently assess when there are no resource available on a search topic.

And third, they seldom carry the full text of any article, book, report, or other document that you identify in their databases. This distinction may again make you question why you would want to access these resources. The answer has two parts: The first is that by searching several comprehensive library indexes and ERIC, you stand a good chance of identifying the key resources related to your topic of inquiry, because at major libraries professional bibliographers are responsible for identifying important works and maintaining up-to-date collections in their field. Second, ERIC is the most comprehensive guide to published and unpublished works in education. Once you identify key authors and titles, you can set out on the Internet to see if any of these works are available. On the Internet you will often find abstracts, partial or full text of newer books and reports, and related works by the same author. Failing that, you have the option of purchasing them (possibly via the Internet), borrowing the references from your local library, or arranging for interlibrary loans.

In this chapter, I describe how you go about accessing and searching these two kinds of bibliographic resources, beginning with libraries.

Accessing and Searching Libraries of the World

Your first challenge in searching world libraries will be to identify the most promising ones to search. Several carefully selected libraries will probably be all you need to access for a comprehensive search on your topic. You will likely want to begin with libraries that are close to you geographically, because you may be more familiar with the extent of their collections and you may have or can arrange to obtain borrowing privileges. Your next stop should be one or two major university research libraries that have strong general collections or reputations for outstanding collections related to your topic, or the Library of Congress, as it houses the largest general library in the United States. If your topic has an international dimension or if it concerns a foreign language or culture, you will also want to try major libraries located in the relevant country.

After giving some thought to which libraries you want to access, you next need to locate their Internet addresses. If it's a university library you're after, you can sometimes make an educated guess at what the institution's home page URL is and then follow the links to the library. For example, using *http://www* as a prefix and *edu* as a suffix, you'll correctly guess Harvard University's URL as *http://www.harvard.edu* and Stanford's as *http://www.stanford.edu*. Other institutions' URLs are not as obvious, especially names that begin with "University of." The University of Texas at Austin, for instance, is *http://www.utexas.edu*, not *http://www.uta.edu*. In this case your best bet is to go to

Yahoo! or one of the other major directories. Under the heading Reference, you'll find links to an extensive array of university and public libraries.

Searching a Library with a Web Gateway

The University of Texas at Austin library, which was among the first of the major research university libraries to offer a Web "gateway" to its catalog of holdings, is typical of what you'll find, and serves as a good example to illustrate Web access. The library can be reached directly by pointing your browser to *http://www.lib.utexas.edu*, or by following links from the university's home page URL given above. At the library's home page, select the link to *UTNetCat*, the name given to its Web-browsable online catalog. You will then see the following screen (Figure 11–1).

Of the four available search options, the last one, *Reserve Lists*, is for use only by students enrolled in courses at the institution. Of the remaining three options, *Keyword* is the one I suggest you choose, because it allows you the most flexibility in searching. *Browse* is only appropriate if you know the exact spelling of an author's name or are familiar with the catalog's subject headings; *Command* allows you to use the same commands needed for Telnet connections.

After selecting *Keyword* from the page, you are presented with a blank search form with space to enter up to four keywords. The keywords may be joined by selecting the

Figure 11–1

119

operators AND, OR, or NOT, just as you saw in the Web search engines. You have the choice of restricting the search to the Author, Title, or Subject fields in the database by making the appropriate choice in the pull-down menu to the left of the blank, or you can choose Mixed, which allows all of these fields to be searched. You can also restrict a search to one of the university's special collections by choosing the collection (e.g., music publisher) from a pull-down menu and entering a keyword.

Let's say you're researching the topic "teaching English with computers." Into the form, enter the three relevant words: "teaching," "English," and "computers." Since you want to retrieve records that contain all of these words, select AND to join them. Some experimentation is needed to determine whether to restrict the search to only certain fields or to do a mixed search. Mixed searches obviously will produce more hits than restricted searches, and they often produce too many hits to deal with. For now, try restricting your search to the Subject field, as shown below, in Figure 11–2.

After selecting *Start KEYWORD Search*, you are presented with the following screen, which informs you that three records were found and supplies their titles (see Figure 11–3).

Figure 11–2

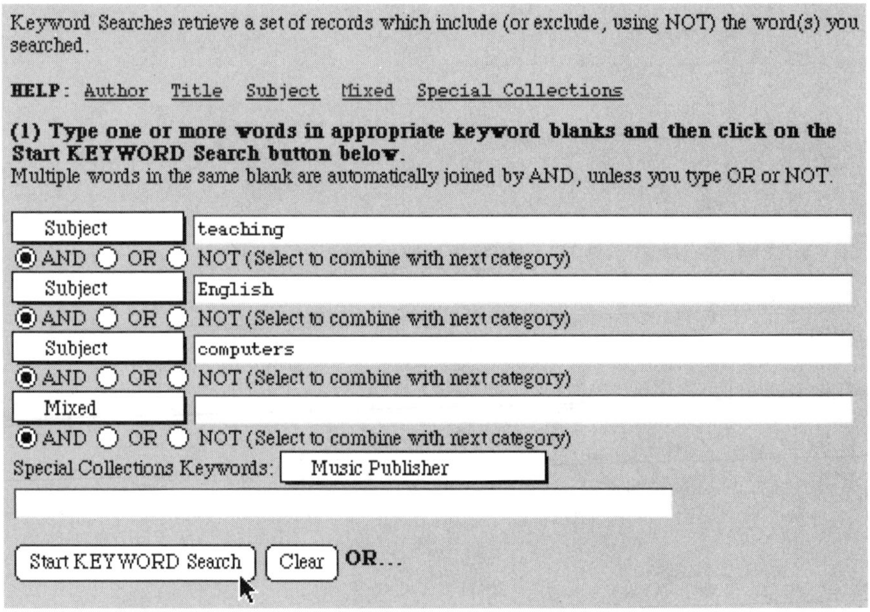

Keyword Searches retrieve a set of records which include (or exclude, using NOT) the word(s) you searched.

HELP: <u>Author</u>   <u>Title</u>   <u>Subject</u>   <u>Mixed</u>   <u>Special Collections</u>

(1) Type one or more words in appropriate keyword blanks and then click on the Start KEYWORD Search button below.
Multiple words in the same blank are automatically joined by AND, unless you type OR or NOT.

Subject	teaching

⦿ AND ◯ OR ◯ NOT (Select to combine with next category)

Subject	English

⦿ AND ◯ OR ◯ NOT (Select to combine with next category)

Subject	computers

⦿ AND ◯ OR ◯ NOT (Select to combine with next category)

Mixed	

⦿ AND ◯ OR ◯ NOT (Select to combine with next category)

Special Collections Keywords: | Music Publisher |

| Start KEYWORD Search | | Clear | **OR...**

Figure 11–3

KEYWORD Search Results Brief Display

**YOUR SEARCH: SK TEACHING AND SK ENGLISH AND SK COMPUTERS
found 3 item(s).**

(Records 1 - 3) For Full Display, click on number.

1 Literacy and computers : the complications of teaching and learning with technology. / New York
/ 1994
LC 149.5 L575 1994 PCL Stacks CHECKED OUT DUE 10/17/96

2 Literacy online : the promise (and peril) of reading and writing with computers. / Pittsburgh /
1992
LC 149.5 L58 1992 PCL Stacks
LC 149.5 L58 1992 PCL Stacks COPY 2 CHECKED OUT DUE 10/17/96
LC 149.5 L58 1992 UGL Reserves

3 Word perfect : literacy in the computer age. / Tuman, Myron C., 1946- / London / 1992
LC 149.5 T8 1992B PCL Stacks CHECKED OUT DUE 10/12/96

End of results for your search.

Note that each title is numbered. Because the numbers are underlined, you know that they are links. To display the full record, click on the number. When you scan the record, as shown below, you can see that the three keywords you searched appear in the subject field (see Figure 11–4).

If you want to expand your search to include more records, you have several options. If you want to find more records similar to that shown, click on the subject line that interests you. This will cause a search on the subject you clicked to be conducted. You can also find references to more works by the same authors by clicking on the authors' names. A third option is to return to the search form and unrestrict your search by choosing Mixed. When I did this, close to five hundred records were retrieved, so in this case you would have to look for more specific keywords to narrow the search. A final option is to try new, but related, keywords such as "literature" or "literacy," and "computers" and keep the search restricted to the subject field.

Searching a Library by Telnet

To contrast what you might expect if the library you want to search does not have a Web interface, I'll illustrate how the search just described would be conducted via a Telnet session. I'm able to do this because the University of Texas offers visitors a

Figure 11–4

FULL DISPLAY

TITLE:
   Literacy and computers : the complications of teaching and learning with technology /
   edited by Cynthia L. Selfe and Susan Hilligoss.
PUBLISHED:
   New York : Modern Language Association of America, 1994.
DESCRIPTION:
   ix, 387 p. : ill. ; 24 cm.
SERIES:
   Research and scholarship in composition 2
NOTES:
   Includes bibliographical references (p. 346-378) and index.
   Contents: Studying literacy with computers / Susan Hilligoss and Cynthia L. Selfe.
SUBJECTS:
   Computers and literacy--United States.
   Language arts--United States--Computer-assisted instruction.
   Reading--United States--Computer-assisted instruction.
   English language--Composition and exercises--Study and teaching--United
   States--Computer-assisted instruction.
OTHER AUTHORS:
   Selfe, Cynthia L., 1951-
   Hilligoss, Susan, 1948-

choice of searching its catalog by Telnet or TN3270, or by the Web. About the only noticeable difference between a Telnet and a TN3270 connection is that TN3270 provides a colored and slightly larger viewing window.

You begin the search by clicking *UTCAT* on the library's home page and then clicking on *Telnet*. Netscape will then launch your Telnet software and, in a small separate window, you'll see the library's greeting message. The message will prompt you to log in with the word "guest." After you do this, you'll see the following screen (see Figure 11–5).

Since you want to search the library catalog, enter "1" and press return. (Remember, your mouse will be of no use while using Telnet.) You will then see the screen in Figure 11–6. To initiate a search, you must enter the one- or two-letter search code obtained from the menu that corresponds with the kind of query you want to do, followed by the search words. Therefore, to search for "teaching English with computers" as subject keywords, you enter "sk teaching English computers" at the bottom of the screen and press return. You will then see exactly the same results as you got when you clicked on *Start KEYWORD Search* at the Web screen. The only difference from a Web search now is that you cannot click on the subject or the authors' names to initiate

Figure 11–5

```
WELCOME TO THE UTCAT LIBRARY INFORMATION SYSTEM
================================================================================

    Work-study positions available NOW; Info class schedule for September;
    UTNetCAT; Remote access; Student address update info - select #8 NEWS

================================================================================
    1  UTCAT LIBRARY CATALOG (books, periodicals, other library materials)

    2  Indexes to ARTICLES in 3600 selected periodicals...
    3  Encyclopedia
    4  Company Directory
    5  Material Safety Data Sheets

    6  Services: RENEW, DUE, EXP, ILS, DOX, PUR
    7  Library hours
    8  UT Library News
    9  UTACCESS Campus Information System
   10  Log off now

    Type the number of your choice, then press ENTER.

-> ■
```

Figure 11–6

```
UTCAT -- SEARCH CHOICES MENU
================================================================================
BROWSE       Author ............  a hemingway ernest
SEARCHES     Title .............  t sun also rises
             Subject ...........  s mexican american authors
             Call number .......  c ps 153 m4 c48 1989

KEYWORD      Author Keyword ....  ak appropriations committee
SEARCHES     Title Keyword .....  tk texas education
             Subject Keyword ...  sk computer security
             Mixed Keyword .....  mk hemingway sun rises

MORE SEARCH CHOICES ...........  press ENTER

RESERVES     INstructor ........  in clarke, s
LISTS        COurse Number .....  co his 389

SERVICES     RENEW, DUE, EXP, ILS, DOX, PUR ...  ser
================================================================================
Type your search (example: tk texas education), then press ENTER,
OR for more examples, type only the search command, then press ENTER
-> sk teaching English computers■
HELp     ? = other commands    MENu = search choices    STOp = main menu
```

another search. Instead, you have to enter your search from scratch. For example, if you wanted more works by the author of the first record in the list, Cynthia Selfe, you would have to type "ak Selfe Cynthia" and press return.

Searching the Library of Congress

Everything I've described so far generally applies to searching all major libraries in the world. However, there is one important exception to searching the Library of Congress. Not all parts of its public databases are searchable with the Web. This is important to know because you'll need to use Telnet or TN3270 if you want to conduct a thorough search. Unfortunately, the Library of Congress is notoriously difficult for the inexperienced user to access via Telnet. Therefore, unless you are prepared to carefully study the online help, I do not recommend you search it this way.

To search the Library of Congress via the Web, point your browser to *http:// lcweb.loc.gov*. Locate the research tools section, and click on the Go button next to the Library of Congress catalogs pull-down selection item. You will then see a page containing two sections of interest: word search and browse search. The first one allows you to search for specific words or numbers in the library's catalogs; the second lets you browse alphabetical indexes of the library's catalogs by author, subject, and title. After you choose the type of search you want to conduct, you will be presented with a form into which you can enter your search terms.

Searching for Research Literature with ERIC

Searching ERIC is essential if you wish to thoroughly research any topic related to teaching, for it indexes over seven hundred education and education-related journals as well as references to unpublished articles, papers, and reports. Unlike the library databases just described, each bibliographic entry in ERIC contains a brief abstract of the item. This is extremely helpful because sometimes the abstract alone gives you sufficient information about your topic. It also prevents wasted time in tracking down a reference whose title sounds interesting, but whose content is not useful for your purposes.

Many Internet sites provide public access to ERIC; go to the Yahoo! *Reference* heading to locate them. You should be aware that many sites require the use of Telnet or TN3270. The site I prefer is AskERIC, maintained by Syracuse University, because it has a convenient Web form for searching. It can be found at *http://ericir.syr.edu/*. Since there are some differences between ERIC and library databases, I'll illustrate how to conduct a search from the AskERIC site.

Suppose you wanted to find out what the well-known MIT author and father of the Logo computer language, Seymour Papert, has written about mathematics and computers. Click on *Search ERIC Database*. Enter the words "Papert Seymour," "mathematics," and "computers" (without the quotes) into the form that appears. Beside each term, notice that there is a pull-down menu from which you select the field you want searched for the term. Since Seymour Papert is an author, you choose Author from the pull-down menu; for the other two terms, select Keyword. I'll explain the other choices in these menus shortly. Next, for the Relation operator, choose "and" because you want all three terms to appear in your search results. You have two other choices, "or" and "not." Finally, if you can, limit the number of records returned by entering a number less than forty at the bottom of the screen. After filling in all relevant blanks, click on *Submit Query* (see Figure 11–7).

You will then be given several records, one of which is illustrated in Figure 11–8.

Figure 11–7

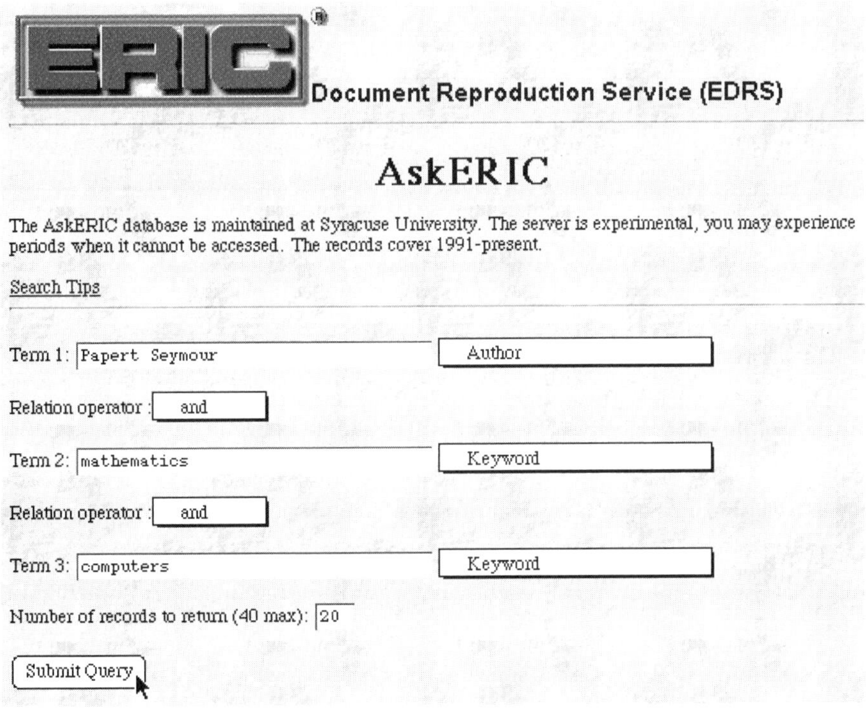

ERIC®
Document Reproduction Service (EDRS)

AskERIC

The AskERIC database is maintained at Syracuse University. The server is experimental, you may experience periods when it cannot be accessed. The records cover 1991-present.

Search Tips

Term 1: Papert Seymour   Author

Relation operator :   and

Term 2: mathematics   Keyword

Relation operator :   and

Term 3: computers   Keyword

Number of records to return (40 max): 20

Submit Query

Figure 11–8

EJ467698
Title: Styles and Voices.
Author: Turkle, Sherry; Papert, Seymour
Journal Citation: For the Learning of Mathematics; v13 n1 p49-52 Feb 1993
Language: English
Descriptors:
Case_Studies
Cognitive_Style
College_Students
Computers
Elementary_Education
Elementary_School_Students
Higher_Education
Individual_Characteristics
Logical_Thinking
Mathematics_Education
Programers
Programing
Psychiatry
Psychology
Sex_Differences
Student_Behavior
Thinking_Skills

Identifiers: LOGO Programing Language
Abstract: Case studies of elementary school and college students are used to examine the different styles of approach taken to computer programing. Introduces the term bricoleur to describe programers who do not take a structured approach to programing. Discusses gender differences among programers. (MDH)
Clearinghouse No.: SE551128
Publication Type: 143; 080
Publication Date: 1993

This record is for an article that appeared in the journal *For the Learning of Mathematics*. You would have to go to a library to get this journal; however, noncopyrighted materials are available from ERIC in microfiche or hard copy form. The record will tell you if the reference is available in these formats and, if it is, you can order it directly from the ERIC Documentation Reproduction Service. To order, you need only select the checkbox that appears at the end of the record and click on *Order* at the bottom of the list of records. You will then be prompted to provide your mailing address and method of payment.

Before you order anything, however, you may want to check your nearest library to see if it houses the ERIC microfiche collection, as many libraries frequented by teachers do. If so, you need to copy down the six-digit ED number that appears at the top of the record to be able to locate the microfiche. Note that the above article is not available from ERIC because its six-digit reference number begins with EJ. This code indicates that the article is from a copyrighted journal. At the end of the record under the Availability heading, there is a note that also informs you of the article's status.

In filling in the search form, I suggested that you select *Keyword* from the pull-down menu. When you make this choice, you'll be telling AskERIC to look for the search terms anywhere on the record. Frequently, keyword searches will produce too many records. If this is the case, you can restrict your search to any of the fields of the record highlighted in bold by making the appropriate choice from the pull-down menu. For example, you could restrict your search to the title field or limit it by publication date. Another option is to restrict your search to the descriptors field. Descriptors are a standard set of labels ERIC uses to classify documents.

ERIC has a unique series of short publications called digests that synthesize research and ideas about emerging issues in education. The full texts (normally about four pages) of most of these summaries are available on the Web. These documents provide an excellent starting point if you are unfamiliar with recent research in your field of interest. If a document is a digest, this word appears in the Identifiers field of the record. Therefore, if you wanted to see if there were any ERIC digests related to mathematics and computers, you'd enter into the search form "mathematics" and "computers" as keywords, and "digests" as an identifier.

Once you identify an interesting digest, you have to go to another Web site to actually view its full text. One such site is at the Office of Educational Research and Improvement of the U.S. Department of Education, *http://www.ed.gov/databases/ERIC_Digests/index/*. In the search form on this page, enter the ED number to retrieve the digest you want.

12 | Finding Other Kinds of Information on the Internet

Although your research tools will likely be confined to those talked about in the last two chapters, there are resources on the Internet that you may not be able to locate with these tools. These are FTP, Gopher, and newsgroup resources. Each of these resources utilizes unique search tools; fortunately, the tools can all be accessed with your Web browser, which greatly simplifies the search task. In this chapter, I'll focus on how to use the search tools for these resources. But first, I'll explain these resources and why you may want to search them.

Why Search FTP, Gopher, and Newsgroups?

Admittedly, with the comprehensive, powerful Web search engines such as AltaVista, HotBot, and Infoseek, there's less and less need to conduct separate searches for FTP, Gopher, and newsgroup resources. More and more sites are making these resources directly available through the Web, and the search engines themselves are capable of retrieving these kinds of non-Web resources. Nevertheless, not all FTP, Gopher, and newsgroup resources can be found with search engines, making it necessary to learn how to use specialized search tools to find these resources. Here's an overview of why you would want to use each these search tools:

- *Finding FTP Resources*. Archie, the special FTP search tool, is best employed when you're looking for hard-to-find software or specific documents of which you know the name but not the location. You'll likely want to use Archie only after a Web search proves unsuccessful; however, there are times when Archie may prove to be more efficient in locating resources. I'll give an example of this in the discussion of Archie below. Generally speaking, Archie is not a good tool to use when you are searching for a concept or have only a general notion of what you're looking for. The Web search engines are far superior for this kind of search. If you are looking specifically for software, there is a Web search service, SHAREWARE.COM, which I'll also describe below, that allows you to search for software using keywords.

• *Finding Gopher Resources.* Veronica is the tool specially designed for locating Gopher resources. Gopher has been largely eclipsed by the Web in the last few years; nonetheless, some older Gopher documents may not be accessible via the Web search engines, necessitating the use of Veronica. This is not a problem, however, because Veronica is very simple to use.

• *Finding Newsgroup Resources.* It's always wise to include newsgroups in your research because they are where you'll find people talking about the latest concepts, ideas, or trends in almost any field. In fact, the Internet newsgroups have been called the largest information utility in the world. Unlike FTP and Gopher, whose future is unclear, newsgroup traffic volume is increasing exponentially. Several of the search engines discussed earlier give you the option of including newsgroups in your search criteria (e.g., AltaVista); however, I recommend the use of DejaNews, a specialized tool for newsgroup searching. The DejaNews database is significantly larger and has a specially designed interface for newsgroup searching.

How to Find FTP Resources with Archie

Let's say I'm a high school English teacher wanting to locate the full text of Shakespeare's play *Hamlet* for my class. I've heard that it's available on the Internet, but I don't know where it can be found. I tried entering "hamlet" into the Web search engine Hotbot, but was I overwhelmed when 47,450 hits came back! The hits on the first page were the home pages of people who liked Hamlet or discussions about Hamlet. Rather than wasting time wading through these pages looking for links to the text of the play, I decided to try Archie. I made the reasonable assumption that the text file would be called "hamlet," although it could have a file extension added on to it.

There are at least five or six Web gateways available to conduct Archie searches. You'll find minor variations among them, but they all function the same way. The best way to locate them is to go to Yahoo! and follow the path from the home page *Computers and Internet: Internet: FTP Sites: Searching: Archie.* Here you'll see a list of links to Archie search forms. Choose one that is geographically close to you (you can tell this by looking at the domain name from the URL) and click on the link. To do the search for *Hamlet*, I chose the University of Illinois Urbana Champaign's Archie gateway, *http://hoohoo.ncsa.uiuc.edu/archie.html.* When I clicked on this link, I saw the screen below, then entered the word "hamlet" into the form (see Figure 12–1).

After entering the search term, I had several options to set. From a pull-down menu, I could choose whether I wanted the search to be case sensitive or insensitive, with the search term being part of a larger term (i.e., a substring), or whether I wanted the search to match exactly with what I entered. I chose the least restrictive search, "Case Insensitive Substring Match." The other options allow you to determine how your search results will be sorted (by host or date), the impact on other users or the priority in which Archie processes your request (don't feel guilty about using the default choice "Not Nice at All"),

Figure 12–1

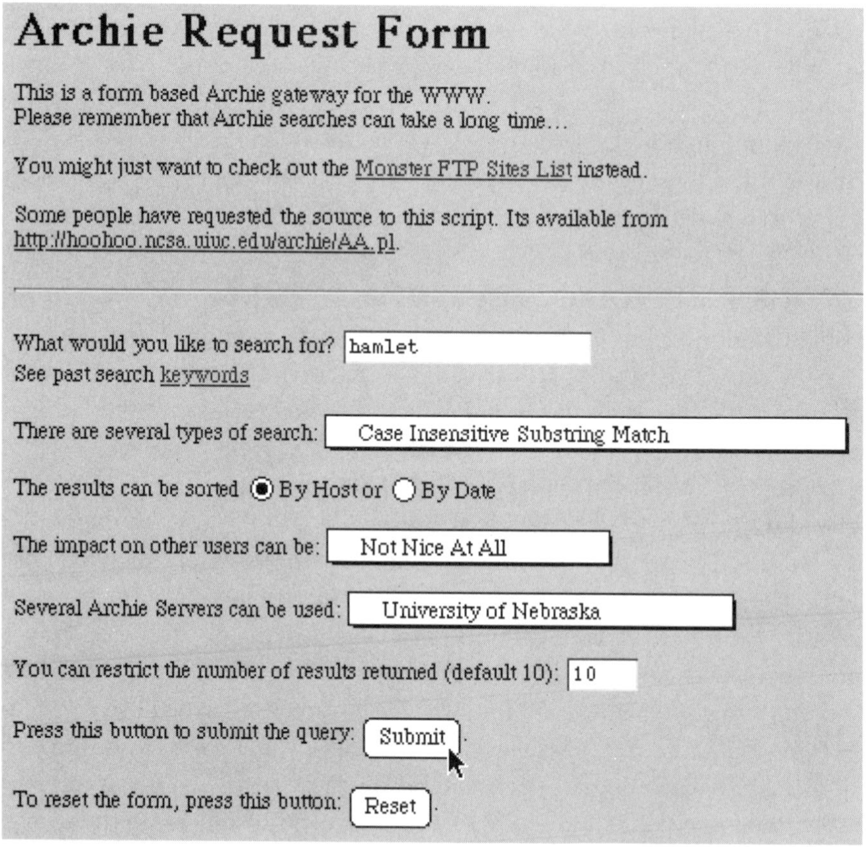

Archie Request Form

This is a form based Archie gateway for the WWW.
Please remember that Archie searches can take a long time...

You might just want to check out the Monster FTP Sites List instead.

Some people have requested the source to this script. Its available from
http://hoohoo.ncsa.uiuc.edu/archie/AA.pl.

What would you like to search for? `hamlet`
See past search keywords

There are several types of search: | Case Insensitive Substring Match |

The results can be sorted ⦿ By Host or ◯ By Date

The impact on other users can be: | Not Nice At All |

Several Archie Servers can be used: | University of Nebraska |

You can restrict the number of results returned (default 10): `10`

Press this button to submit the query: | Submit |

To reset the form, press this button: | Reset |

the server you want to use (choose one that is close to you geographically), and the number of hits to be returned. Once I made my choices, I clicked on *Submit.*

At the top of the Archie search form, you are warned that a search can take a long time. Normally, Archie doesn't take much longer than a slow Web search engine. However, at busy times you may have to wait a minute or two for your results. Below is an excerpt of the list of results I obtained from my search. You'll see the name of the host that has the document, the directory (or folder) in which the requested document is located, and the file itself, with an indication of its size and date (see Figure 12–2). When you click on the file name, it will be downloaded to your computer.

In many cases, you'll find FTP text files have the extension "Z" or "PDF." Z indicates that the file has been compressed using a UNIX compression technique; PDF indicates that the file is in Adobe Acrobat format. Acrobat is an increasingly popular file format because it allows all the special formatting of documents to be preserved no matter what type of computer the file is viewed with. Before you can view these, or any

Figure 12–2

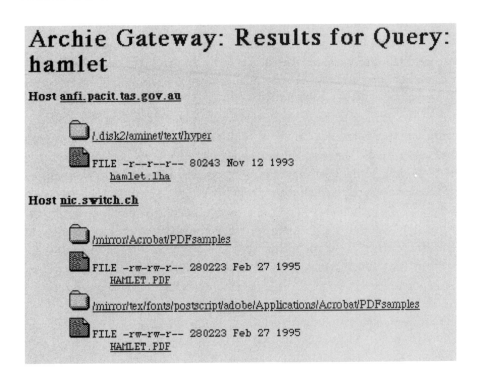

131

other special file types, Netscape has to be configured with the appropriate helper software. You should ask your computer-support person how to do this, as it is beyond the scope of this book to explain it. If Netscape isn't set up to view the type of file that you have, you can look down your results list for a file ending with ".txt" (e.g., *hamlet.txt*) or with just the search term itself (e.g., hamlet). These files are in ordinary text format and can be viewed directly in your word processor after they are downloaded.

The same principles apply to searching for software. For example, if you wanted to find the latest version of Disinfectant, the popular Macintosh antivirus software, but didn't know the version number, you would just conduct a case-insensitive substring search for the word "disinfectant." Once you get back your list of hits, you would then scan the list for the highest version number and date and download it. Again, software will often be found in special compressed formats, such as "zip" for Windows and "sit" for Macintosh, so Netscape needs to be configured with the corresponding helper utility to expand the software. You will need to do this not only when downloading from sites found by Archie, but when you download software from Web sites.

Searching for Software

If you're looking for software that will help you with your classroom teaching or with your own personal productivity, the Web searching engines and Archie will definitely be of use. However, if you're looking for software on a certain topic, the most efficient service is SHAREWARE.COM, hosted by CNET (*www.cnet.com*). At this site you'll find some two hundred thousand files of freeware, shareware, demos, fixes, patches, and upgrades for all popular computer platforms. This service has several advantages over Archie and the Web search engines. When you locate the software you want, you're given a choice of sites to download it from, and these sites have reliability ratings. You can also conveniently search for software by keyword and computer platform, and the site is very up to date.

To access SHAREWARE.COM, point your browser to *http://www.shareware.com*. From the site's home page, you're given a choice of three types of searches, Quick, Simple, and Power, each of which gives you progressively more control over search options. In performing a Simple search for problem-solving software, you would first click on *Simple Search* from the home page. You'd then see the easy-to-use form in Figure 12–3.

Enter "problem" and "solving" as keywords and check the "and" box in step 1. In step 2 choose the computer platform from the pull-down menu (I chose All Categories). Step 3 allows you to specify the maximum number of hits displayed on a page or accept the default number of twenty-five. Finally, in step 4, click on *start search*. Below is a description of the first item that was found (see Figure 12–4). To download the software, you need only click on the software file name and then select the site that you want to download it from. The list of sites is ordered by country; beside each is its downloading reliability rating.

Figure 12–3

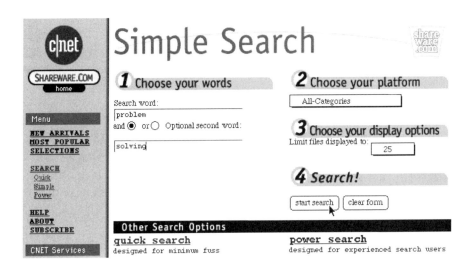

Figure 12–4

Search Results

File Platform: **All-Categories**
Description or file matches: **problem solving**
Search **is not case sensitive**
Files per page: **25**

**Files from the uni-mac archive
(since Aug 22,19122)**

onslaughtdemo1.02.cpt.hqx
**game/demo/
Jun 21,1995
908 K**

Really good, really original games are few and far between, but this one is both. You are a marble and, well, it's hard to describe what you have to do. Something on the order of bouncing into blocks and making sure you knock two blocks open of the same color. Suffice it to say, however, that the feel and the animation are both excellent, you can play in color or in black & white, by yourself or with another person on a network with a Mac, NeXT or Atari box. Incorporates elements of **problem solving** and dexterity. Wonderful! You can only do the first 10 levels without paying for the instruction book.

From this example, you can see that this site's sheer simplicity, coupled with the richness of its resources, makes SHAREWARE.COM a highly attractive first stop in your search for software. When I tried to search for problem-solving software with the major Web search engines, I was able to locate some only after spending a considerable amount of time. This was because I had to try various combinations of keywords and because searches typically produced several hundred hits, so it was necessary to sift through many documents before finding some with actual software to download.

How to Find Gopher Resources with Veronica

To locate the full text of Hamlet as a Gopher resource, using Veronica, return to Yahoo! and follow the path from the home page *Computers and Internet: Internet: Gopher: Searching: Veronica*. When you do this, you'll see a list of about a dozen different links to Veronica. I chose the University of Reno link, which took me to the URL *gopher:// veronica.scs.unr.edu/11/veronica*. I then saw the menu in Figure 12–5.

This menu provides two choices for locating resources: *Find Gopher directories* and *Search GopherSpace*. If you select the former, you'll find only directories named Hamlet, which may or may not contain the actual text of the play. On the other hand, if you select *Search GopherSpace*, you'll be searching for both directories and document titles named Hamlet. I decided to choose the latter, since it is the most comprehensive search type. It doesn't matter which of the three Veronica sites you search first, U. Nac. Autonoma de MX, PSINet, or NYSERNet. If you can't find what you want at one site, or if one is busy, then try another. In theory, the sites should be identical, because they are supposed to contain indexes to all public Gopher sites in the world. In practice, however, you will find differences in their contents, as they are updated at different times.

When I clicked on PSINet, a search form appeared, into which I entered the keyword "hamlet." After pressing the return key, I was provided with a list of documents and directories, part of which is shown in Figure 12–6. When I clicked on the Hamlet directory, the third item in the list, I was shown a list of documents. Each document comprised an act of the play. To read any document, you must click on the document name. Unlike FTP, where you have to download a document before you can view it, Gopher allows you immediate access as soon as you click on it.

Gopher does not have the same flexibility as the major Web search engines for conducting advanced searches. You can, however, conduct Boolean searches, and the asterisk (*) can be used as a wild card at the end of a search string. For further details on how to conduct Veronica searches, click on the *how-to-query-veronica* and the *veronica-faq* documents in the main Gopher menu.

Figure 12–5

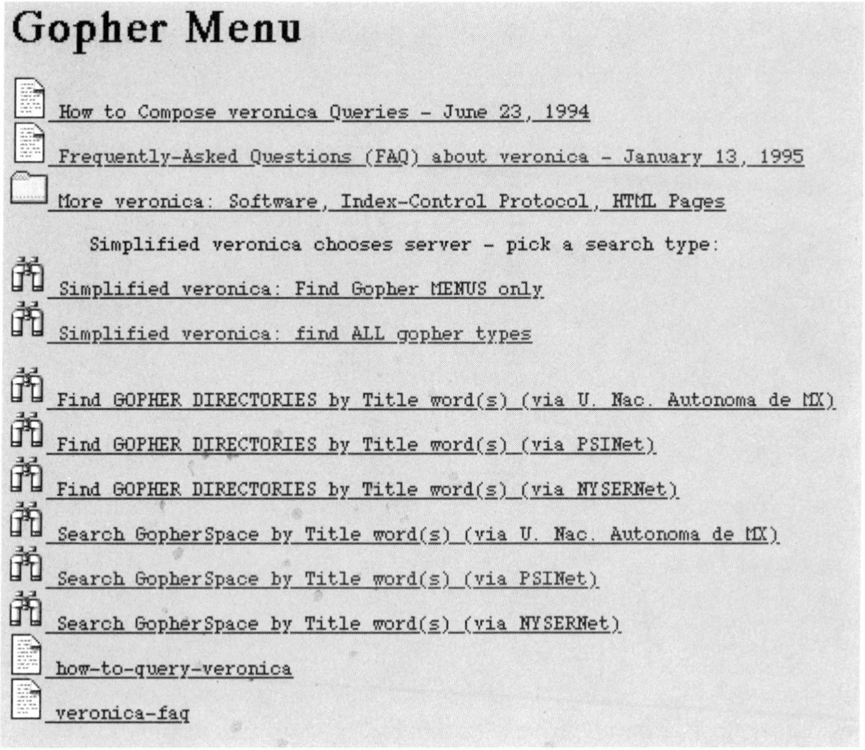

Gopher Menu

How to Compose veronica Queries – June 23, 1994

Frequently-Asked Questions (FAQ) about veronica – January 13, 1995

More veronica: Software, Index-Control Protocol, HTML Pages

   Simplified veronica chooses server – pick a search type:

Simplified veronica: Find Gopher MENUS only

Simplified veronica: find ALL gopher types

Find GOPHER DIRECTORIES by Title word(s) (via U. Nac. Autonoma de MX)

Find GOPHER DIRECTORIES by Title word(s) (via PSINet)

Find GOPHER DIRECTORIES by Title word(s) (via NYSERNet)

Search GopherSpace by Title word(s) (via U. Nac. Autonoma de MX)

Search GopherSpace by Title word(s) (via PSINet)

Search GopherSpace by Title word(s) (via NYSERNet)

how-to-query-veronica

veronica-faq

Figure 12–6

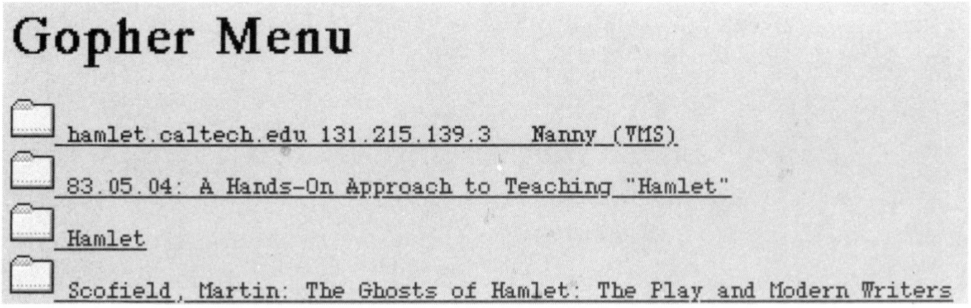

Gopher Menu

hamlet.caltech.edu 131.215.139.3   Nanny (VMS)

83.05.04: A Hands-On Approach to Teaching "Hamlet"

Hamlet

Scofield, Martin: The Ghosts of Hamlet: The Play and Modern Writers

How to Find Newsgroup Resources

Most of the major search engines discussed in Chapter 10 allow you to search newsgroups, although none are as comprehensive or elegant to use as DejaNews. This specialized search tool archives postings to most of the twenty thousand newsgroups in existence from March 1995 onward. When you consider that over 500 megabytes, or the equivalent of five hundred hefty, four-hundred-page novels, are posted to newsgroups every single day of the year, DejaNews' database is gigantic. Furthermore, DejaNews is committed to archiving as far back as 1979, when the Usenet newsgroup system first began, a massive undertaking. Once you become familiar with this tool, you'll definitely want to return to it in your research.

In demonstrating how to use DejaNews, I'll continue my example of the high school English teacher. Let's say I decided to broaden my search to see what resources I could find for teaching high school English. More specifically, I thought I'd see if anyone has inquired about or discussed lesson plans on teaching English literature. I began by pointing my browser to the DejaNews home page at *http://www.dejanews.com*. At this page you'll see a search form into which you can enter any terms in order to conduct a simple search. This type of search will examine only the most recent newsgroup archives, so right away I decided to click on *Power Search*, because I wanted to search the full DejaNews archives. Into the search form, I entered

> lesson plans "high school" english

In general, the search language used by DejaNews is similar to that of the major Web search engines. I put quotes around *high school* so that the two words would be searched for as a unit, and I didn't put anything between the words, as DejaNews assumes that they are connected by "and" unless you tell it otherwise. Under search options, I selected the "old" Usenet Database, which is much larger than the "current" one. I left the other options at the default settings, but as you can see from the form below there are many ways that you can custom tailor your search (see Figure 12–7).

After clicking on *Find*, I received back a list of seventy-one hits, with twenty-five appearing on the first page (see Figure 12–8). The list is in order of the score an article receives on the search terms I used; however, you can see from the search options that other sortings are possible.

The last item on the list of hits appeared promising for two reasons: (1) the words "Lesson Plan Ideas" are central to my interest, and (2) the word "Re:" indicates that the newsgroup article is a response to another posting about lesson plans, which suggests that there has been some discussion on the topic. When I clicked on *Re: Lesson Plan Ideas on*, I saw the article shown in Figure 12–9.

Sure enough, what we see is a response from "Andy" to an article that "Jim" had posted requesting help to identify Web and FTP sites that had high school literature

Figure 12–7

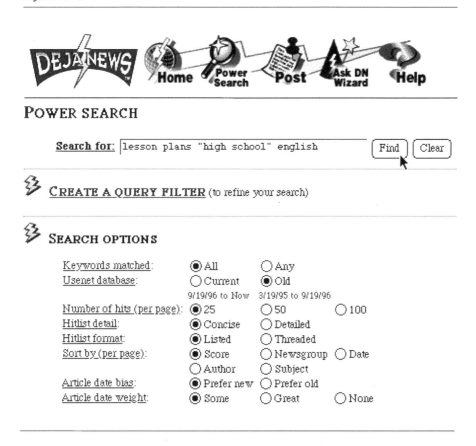

POWER SEARCH

Search for: `lesson plans "high school" english`   [Find]   [Clear]

CREATE A QUERY FILTER (to refine your search)

SEARCH OPTIONS

Keywords matched:	⦿ All	◯ Any	
Usenet database:	◯ Current	⦿ Old	
	9/19/96 to Now	3/19/95 to 9/19/96	
Number of hits (per page):	⦿ 25	◯ 50	◯ 100
Hitlist detail:	⦿ Concise	◯ Detailed	
Hitlist format:	⦿ Listed	◯ Threaded	
Sort by (per page):	⦿ Score	◯ Newsgroup	◯ Date
	◯ Author	◯ Subject	
Article date bias:	⦿ Prefer new	◯ Prefer old	
Article date weight:	⦿ Some	◯ Great	◯ None

lesson plans. Andy's response contains a Web site to check out. Note that the URL of this site (*http://www.rmplc.co.uk/orgs/bln/*) is underlined. This means it's a hypertext link, so you can immediately click on it and view the site Andy recommended!

At the top left of this message, you'll see navigation buttons that allow you to move to the next or previous article in the list of seventy-one retrieved articles, and next to these is a button to return back to the list generated by your search. The fourth button will take you to a list of articles dealing with the same subject as the article you are currently viewing. When I clicked on this button I saw the list in Figure 12–10.

At the top of this list is Jim's original posting and below it is Andy's reply. You know it's a reply because it is indented. Underneath Andy's reply is a reply to his article by "Keith." There is also another reply to Jim from "Dave." When I clicked on Keith's response, I saw that he suggested some more Web sites for Jim to investigate.

Figure 12–8

Hits **1-25** of 71 for Query: **lesson plans "high school" english**

	Date	Scr	Subject	Newsgroup	Author
1.	95/12/06	070	Need High School English	k12.chat.teacher	Ramona DeRyan <dery
2.	95/10/17	070	BLOCK SCHEDULING HIGH SC	misc.education	Paul and Susan Hutc
3.	96/06/16	067	Lesson Plans for the upc	alt.teachers.lesson	James Noll <janoll@
4.	96/08/02	065	Searching for versions o	rec.arts.books.chil	aosterwe@newshost.l
5.	96/03/03	064	Re: Teaching RJ (a view	humanities.lit.auth	James Eason <jeason
6.	96/07/19	063	QL lesson plans	rec.arts.sf.tv.quan	Liz Daniell <ldanie
7.	96/07/18	063	Re: YKYAOLW...	rec.arts.sf.tv.quan	Liz Daniell <ldanie
8.	96/06/01	062	Re: alternative schedule	k12.chat.teacher	Roger Schoenstein <
9.	95/06/05	062	Re: Shakespeare	k12.lang.art	st-arnld@st-arnld.m
10.	96/01/30	061	Re: Block Scheduling	k12.chat.teacher	Roger Schoenstein <
11.	95/08/08	061	"Teaching" Creativity	k12.chat.teacher	meprod@cyber1.servt
12.	96/09/09	060	Resume for Trainer, #1/2	seattle.jobs.wanted	roryo@aa.net (roryo
13.	95/09/23	060	Wanted: Crash Course in	ny.wanted	adp5306@is.nyu.edu
14.	96/08/06	059	Re: Searching for versio	rec.arts.books.chil	cccandc@alaska.net
15.	96/06/07	059	ESL materials, Lesson Pl	soc.culture.korean	idavidso@calvin.ste
16.	96/05/28	059	Advice needed	k12.ed.science	klawler@ior.com (Ke
17.	96/04/27	059	Re: Block Scheduling	schl.sig.k12admin	Roger Schoenstein <
18.	96/04/05	059	Re: block scheduling	k12.chat.teacher	Roger Schoenstein <
19.	96/09/07	058	Re: Stimson Wrench	sci.engr.electrical	hobdbcgv@aol.com (H
20.	96/08/08	058	Resume: Software Tra#1/2	seattle.jobs.wanted	roryo@aa.net (Micha
21.	96/07/25	058	HELP: MUSICAL lesson pla	rec.arts.theatre.mu	Liz Daniell <ldanie
22.	96/04/18	058	Re: Question that needs	schl.sig.k12admin	Anna Nalewajka <RCH
23.	96/01/10	058	Re: Block Sceduling Help	misc.education	Roger Schoenstein <
24.	95/07/20	058	Re: Business Teachers ?	k12.ed.business	bucks@rmii.com (Buc
25.	96/01/23	057	Re: Lesson Plan Ideas on	alt.books.reviews	acox@mail.rmplc.co.

Get next 25 hits

To the right of the *Thread* button is the *Author Profile* button. If you click on this button, you'll retrieve a list of all of the postings in DejaNews' database that the author of an article (Jim, in the first example) has made. This is especially useful if you come across an author who seems particularly knowledgeable about a topic and want to follow up on what this person has written about on other occasions. The other three buttons allow you to post a reply to any article to the same newsgroups it originated from, post a new article to these groups, or e-mail a reply directly to the author of an article.

Other Features of DejaNews

So far I've shown how DejaNews can be used as a powerful search tool for tracking down newsgroup articles containing keywords you provide. There are three other attractive features of DejaNews that also deserve mention:

• *Query Filter.* When you click on *Create a Query Filter* on the DejaNews Power Search page, you are taken to a form for creating a filter that allows you to restrict your searches according to criteria you specify. You can fill in the names of newsgroups that you would like to restrict your search to, and if you're not certain which groups to include, you can browse a hierarchical

Figure 12–9

Article 25 of 71

```
Subject:      Re: Lesson Plan Ideas on Net...WHERE?
From:         acox@mail.rmplc.co.uk (Andy Cox)
Date:         1996/01/23
Message-Id:   <4e3aq2$qq0@spider.rmplc.co.uk>
References:   <4dmgrj$17s@pacifier.com>
Organization: News item provided from RM News Server.
Newsgroups:   alt.books.reviews,alt.usage.english,misc.education,misc.education.la
```

jimc@pacifier.com (Jim Connett) wrote:

check out BLN Online at:

http://www.rmplc.co.uk/orgs/bln/

lots of stuff

Andy Cox

```
>I have a quick question for anyone who wishes to answer.
>
>I have been searching the net for sites (both FTP as well as WWW) that provide teaching
>ideas/lesson plans for High School Literature.  Does anyone know of any sites that offer
>these teaching aides?
>
>If you have any information that might help me in my search, if you would be so kind as
>to directly e-mail them to me, I would appreciate it (jimc@pacifier.com).  I don't get into my
>newsreader as often as I get into e-mail.
>
>Thanks to one and all.
```

Figure 12–10

Lesson Plan Ideas on Net...WHERE? - jimc@pacifier.com (Jim Connett)
   o acox@mail.rmplc.co.uk (Andy Cox)
        □ Keith Turner
   o dmoorman@interaccess.com (Dave Moorman)

list of available groups to identify those that you'd like to include in the filter. The filter also allows you to specify newsgroup dates, authors, and subjects to narrow your search even further. Once you have specified your filter criteria, when you do a power search the filter is used until you request that it be cleared. The query filter is a real time-saver, especially if you are doing multiple searches on different topics with the same newsgroups.

- *Query Profile.* With the large number of newsgroups in existence, one of the biggest challenges you face when using them is identifying which of the groups deal with topics that interest you. The *Query Profile*, an option that is accessed via the *Features* link on the home page of DejaNews, provides a way to help with this task. When you enter keywords reflecting your topics of interest, DejaNews returns an ordered list of newsgroups where your keywords appear often. Beside the list of group names is a score indicating the level of confidence that the keywords are present in the corresponding group. You can select any group from this list to add to a query filter as well.

- *Read Newsgroups.* As you might have already imagined, DejaNews is itself a fully functioning, easy-to-use newsreader. This means that you don't have to bother using separate newsreader software—you can read, post, and reply to news articles right from DejaNews. There are two reasons why you might want to take advantage of this feature. First, you may not have access to a news server and therefore are unable to make use of the resource at all. DejaNews gives you that access. Second, very few servers carry all newsgroups, so it may turn out that groups you want to subscribe to are not available. As I mentioned earlier in this book, the server at my university does not carry *k-12* or *schl*, two major school-related newsgroups. Fortunately, DejaNews carries most of the groups in existence, even obscure groups such as *rel.com* from Russia. You can now see how futile it is to censor certain offensive newsgroups, because if your Internet provider blocks a group, you can always go to DejaNews to get it!

How DejaNews Compares with Web Search Engines

Earlier in this chapter, I mentioned that DejaNews has a significantly larger database of newsgroups than the Web search engines. To give you an example of the difference, I entered my surname (which is relatively obscure) into all of the search engines described in Chapter 10 that provide the capability of newsgroups searches. None of them produced any hits. When I did this with DejaNews, seven hits were produced in the new section of the database and eighty-eight in the old section, including all of the postings that I made after March 1995. Try your own surname—or any other term—and see how DejaNews compares.

If this simple test has any validity, DejaNews wins hands down. I do not even bother using the newsgroup search features of the Web engines, but turn to DejaNews whenever I'm interested in finding out what's been said about a topic in the newsgroups.

13

Devising an Internet Research Strategy

The previous three chapters introduced you to the major tools for carrying out research on the Internet: Web search indexes and directories, specialized database search tools, and FTP, Gopher, and newsgroup tools. The tools themselves are not particularly difficult to master. The challenge, however, is to tie what you've learned about the tools together with your research goals, so that you can locate the information you need. In using the Internet for professional development, you will need to locate information that will help you achieve the goals set out in your action plan. There are no hard and fast rules for doing this. Instead, you have to devise some general strategies for tracking down material that will be of use to you. These strategies should take into account both the nature of the information you're seeking and your comfort level, likes, and dislikes with respect to using the search tools available. In this chapter, I'm going to suggest some general guidelines to assist you in this process. After reading these guidelines, I encourage you to adapt them to suit your unique needs.

What Kind of Information Do You Want?

Before beginning to search the Internet, you need to ask yourself, "What kinds of information do I want?" Take a look again at the research questions in the model professional-development action plan in Chapter 4, and if you've written one yourself, review your own research questions. When you do this, you'll see that your questions likely deal with three kinds of information: specific information, Internet resources, and bibliographic resources.

Specific Information

Some research questions require definite, often factual, answers. For example, in the model action plan in Chapter 4 the following questions were posed:

- Are there any university mathematics-education courses offered online?
- Is there any computer software available that helps students develop estimation skills?
- Does the National Council of Teachers of Mathematics (NCTM) have a Web site . . . ?

These questions lead to specific information. The first question encourages you to compile a list of mathematics courses, the second to locate estimation-skills software, and the third to determine whether or not NCTM has a Web site. To answer questions of this kind, you must be able to cast a broad net. Therefore, your research strategy must include the use of search tools that cover the greatest range of Internet resources.

Internet Resource Sites

This category of information responds to broader, more open-ended questions that require the identification of Internet resource sites. When you set out to research these questions, you are uncertain about what, if any, resources you'll find. The following questions from the model action plan fall into this category:

- What Web sites should I monitor regularly for mathematics-education trends, issues, and developments?
- How can I systematically study my own teaching with the goal of trying to improve it?

The first question requires the identification of first-rate Web sites dealing with mathematics education, while the second concerns finding Web sites focusing on, for example, the teacher as researcher. Depending on your focus of study, other resource questions might be: Are there any good sites containing geographic or weather maps? Special education resources? English-as-a-second-language teaching materials? Social studies lesson plans? Your strategy for finding these resources will involve looking for sites hosted by or linked to highly credible organizations or institutions, or searching for sites that are evaluated or recommended by people or organizations you trust.

Bibliographic Resources

This kind of information requires the compilation of lists of articles, research reports and abstracts, position papers, conference proceedings, and other similar kinds of documents. The purpose of compiling these lists, of course, is to learn more about a topic of interest. For example, in our action plan the following questions were asked:

- How can I make math relate more to students' lives?
- How do I find out what researchers and other authors have said about the topic [of motivating students to learn mathematics]?

Other questions might be: What are the barriers to girls learning science? How does the phonics approach to teaching reading compare to the whole language approach? How can I best make use of the computer when I have only one in my classroom? What is common to all of these questions is that (1) you are bound to find many different opinions on the topics, (2) their answers will come from a variety of different Internet sources (Web, Telnet, FTP, Gopher, and newsgroups), and (3) the questions tend to be very open-ended. When you search for this kind of information you will typically bookmark all of the Web resources you find for later reading, and make a written note of non-Web resources for follow-up.

How to Find Specific Information

When you're looking for specific information, I suggest the following strategy:

Step 1. Begin by using one of the more comprehensive search indexes.

By "comprehensive search index," I mean an index that is built specifically to include as many up-to-date Web resources as possible. In this category, I would include AltaVista, HotBot, Lycos, and Infoseek. Often you will find the very first search you attempt will retrieve the documents that will answer your question. The only exception to this suggestion involves looking for software. For software searches, first go to SHAREWARE.COM. If that site doesn't have what you want, then try the search index.

Step 2. Try another search index if you are not successful.

If your search comes up empty, I recommend that you immediately switch to another comprehensive search index and retry the search using the same search keywords. Try one or two more search indexes if you are unsuccessful.

Step 3. Revise your keywords and redo the search if necessary.

After trying several revised keywords, switch to another search index and redo the search with the same combination of keywords. Once you start doing this, you need to keep a record of what search index you've tried and what keywords you've used, otherwise you'll end up forgetting what you've done and wasting time needlessly. I'll talk more about how to choose the right keywords later in the chapter.

Step 4. Try a Newsgroup search.

If the search indexes aren't able to turn up what you need, try searching the newsgroups with DejaNews. Don't bother using the newsgroup search option in the comprehensive search indexes—they simply aren't as good. The result of a newsgroup search won't be an actual link to a resource. What you'll probably find is someone discussing the topic, and possibly mentioning the URLs of Web sites dealing with that topic.

Step 5. Try other specialized search tools.

The final step if none of the above strategies is successful is to try either Archie for FTP resources, or Gopher for older documents.

Example of the Strategy

I wanted to find out if the National Council of Teachers of Mathematics had a Web site. I entered "National Council of Teachers of Mathematics" (with the quotes) into Infoseek. A long list of hits was returned, but after scanning the first two pages, none of them seemed to refer directly to NCTM's home page. I didn't feel it was worth my effort to continue scanning beyond two pages of hits, because those hits would be less relevant. To my surprise I got the same disappointing results with Lycos and AltaVista. I started to think that maybe NCTM didn't have a site, but then I tried HotBot. Sure enough, there was the link to NCTM home page (*http://www.nctm.org*) right on the first page of my search results.

How to Find Internet Resource Sites

The steps for locating Internet resource sites are significantly different from those of tracking down specific resources. A chief difference is that it's an ongoing process. You are finished only when you feel you've found enough good resources to meet your needs. That's because there is no right or wrong answer to this kind of search. Here are the steps that I recommend to find Internet resource sites:

Step 1. Start with Yahoo!

Yahoo! is very comprehensive and up-to-date, so if there's a new site just starting up, the developers will probably first submit it to Yahoo! to publicize it. You will likely want to go down at least one level in Yahoo's directory (e.g., Education) and then do a search for the topic that interests you within that directory. This will prevent receiving too many irrelevant hits. Remember that Yahoo! indexes only titles of Web pages, so there is no point in trying to do a complicated keyword search. Use only one or two nouns as keywords.

Yahoo! will provide you with a very complete list of resource sites to visit related to your area of interest; however, you may find that there are too many to sort through. That's when guidance is needed and it's time to go on to the next step.

Step 2. Try Magellan's and Lycos' rated sites.

As you saw in the search index chapter, Magellan and Lycos have comprehensive data-bases of rated and reviewed sites. These databases are particularly useful in "separating the wheat from the chaff." I recommend first going to Magellan and then immediately conducting an advanced search of "rated and reviewed" sites, specifying that you want to search only for sites that are rated three or four stars.

Next you should go to Lycos. You can't search their rated sites, so you should select *Top 5% Sites* and follow down their subject tree until you find a category that matches your needs. You then need to browse the list of sites you are presented with. Note that you can sort the list of hits according to any one of the criteria on the rated sites.

Step 3. Go to the Argus Clearinghouse and the World Wide Web Virtual Library.

As you saw earlier, these sites are directories to Internet resources. All you need to do is follow down their subject trees until you reach the area that interests you. The strength of these sites is that their resource lists are maintained by professionals in each field of study around the world. I prefer to start with the Argus list, simply because it's slightly easier to use, and then move on to the Virtual Library if I don't find what I need at Argus.

Step 4. Try a search index if you still need more sites.

Search indexes are not the tool of choice for locating resource sites. It's not that they can't retrieve them—they simply return too many hits when you use fairly general key-words. For that reason, I recommend using them for this category of search only if you're not satisfied with the results obtained with the first three steps.

Example

One of the goals of the sample action plan was to find worthwhile sites to monitor reg-ularly for mathematics-education trends, issues, and developments. When I applied the above strategy, I found that searching Yahoo! for mathematics within the k–12 educa-tion subdirectory did not produce very favorable results. The list of sites just didn't seem to be very appealing and I had a feeling that "something was missing." Therefore, I went to Magellan and Lycos and was particularly impressed with the results Magellan produced. Magellan's four-star sites, retrieved from a search of "mathematics education," were extremely rich: university centers focusing on mathematics education, professional associations, and nonprofit projects dedicated to improving the teaching of mathematics. Although I felt I had enough good links to sites, I went to the Argus Clearinghouse and was also impressed that it, too, had additional resources that appeared to be of high quality. To confirm my suspicion that a search index would not be useful, I entered "mathematics education" into AltaVista. It produced ten thousand hits, a few of which on the first several pages looked promising. On the whole, however, the effort was not very fruitful in light of what I had already found.

How to Find Bibliographic Resources

Finding bibliographic resources is perhaps the most challenging and time-consuming information search. I say this not to discourage you, but to warn you that you may reach dead ends along the way, just as any experienced bibliographic searcher might. To avoid carrying out redundant searches, I strongly urge you to keep an accurate written record of the searches you've conducted. Before you even turn to the Internet, try developing a good list of keywords that will precisely describe your topic. The list will likely contain at least several different combinations of keywords joined by Boolean operators. The discussion below on choosing the right keywords will help you with this. After you've got your list, try the following strategy:

Step 1. Begin with a comprehensive search index.

I prefer to start with Infoseek because of its ability to search for synonyms and variants on the roots of your search terms. Work through your list of search terms, making sure to bookmark those terms that produce good results.

Step 2. Repeat your search with several other search indexes.

This is the same strategy as I suggested above for finding specific information, as no two search indexes will turn up the same list of results even when identical search terms are used. From the relevant items you discover during both this step and step 1, your bibliography should now begin to take shape.

Step 3. Search the ERIC database of educational research.

ERIC is an essential stop when researching a topic for the purpose of building a bibliography of readings. It's very current, covers the key journals in education, and is the only central source for scores of unpublished papers, documents, and reports. Use the same keywords you had success with in the search indexes, but remember that ERIC does not offer the rich search language that the sophisticated search indexes feature. Most of the items you retrieve from ERIC will only be abstracts of the originals. You then need to track down the journal or order the hardcopy item from ERIC Document Reproduction Service.

Step 4. Search one or two major research libraries.

Unfortunately, libraries seldom have even abstracts of items referenced in their databases, let alone their full text, although this is starting to change at some libraries. Therefore, as I mentioned when I discussed how to search library databases, you may actually need to borrow the book, report, or other item. You will recall that another strategy I suggested is that once you identify relevant authors and titles, you can use the search indexes to see if the same or other relevant works by the author can be found on the Internet. This same strategy can be used, of course, for items found in ERIC.

Step 5. Do a search of newsgroups to see what's hot.

Newsgroups can be an outstanding source of the latest announcements, ideas, and discussions on almost any imaginable topic. So if you truly want to be up-to-date, your bibliographic search should end with a DejaNews search. Again, use the same search terms as before, paying attention to the expanded search options offered by DejaNews.

Example

I decided to see what kind of reading list I could build on the topic of "motivating children to want to learn mathematics," one of the sample action-plan questions. I began by entering "+mathematics +motivation" (without quotes) into Infoseek. An extremely long list of hits was returned. Scanning the list, I quickly realized that I needed to restrict the search to children, since many references were to college students. Therefore, I added +children to the search string, and retried it. A fairly relevant list of hits was returned and I bookmarked several that were worth pursuing. Next, I tried the same search string with AltaVista, Lycos, and HotBot. The latter returned the best list of hits by far.

After bookmarking a list of about a dozen Web documents, I turned to ERIC. As expected, I found many pertinent articles, whose abstracts I copied and pasted into my word processor for later reference. Then I turned to my own university's library, which I knew had a strong mathematics collection. I looked for titles published over the last few years, still using the same keywords. I copied and pasted the references of these too. The title of one of the books at the top of the library hit list, *Talking Mathematics* (1996), sounded intriguing. I wanted to find out more about the book, so I returned to HotBot and did a search on the title. I found a good abstract of the book at the publisher's Web site; however, no sample chapters were included.

Finally, I went to DejaNews and did a search on the same keywords. After browsing the list of hits, I discovered a fascinating ongoing discussion on the topic in the group *geometry.pre-College*. To my surprise, one of the contributors was a colleague from my university's mathematics department. You never know what fascinating gems you'll unearth when searching newsgroups, but you have to make sure that, in accessing them, you don't get sidetracked from your main purpose.

A Word on Keywords and Syntax

Choosing the right keywords and using the correct syntax to connect them is essential for a successful search, no matter what search tool you use. Your goal should be to produce a list of hits that contains the topic you are looking for on either the first or second page of the list; otherwise, you'll end up spending needless time wading through seemingly endless pages of hits. Many of the search tools contain valuable information in their Help pages on how to improve your searches. Make sure to consult these. Here are some hints, however, that should apply to almost all search tools:

- *Begin by typing a short phrase.* Try to think of several words that unambiguously describe your topic, such as "pythagorean theorem," "dyslexic children," "antiracist education," "whole language teaching," and "mathematics error analysis." You should force the search indexes to look for these words as a phrase, rather than individually. You'll recall that putting the phase in quotes is the normal way of linking words in most search tools; others may provide a pull-down menu to select this option.

- *Take advantage of Boolean operators.* Many beginning users shy away from Boolean operators because they seem too complicated. A little effort in understanding how they work will pay off in yielding more accurate searches. The three most important operators are "AND," "OR," and "NOT." Remember that using "AND" between two words in a search means that the search is to retrieve only documents that contain *both* words; "OR" instructs the search to retrieve documents containing *either* word; and "NOT" instructs the search to retrieve documents that *do not* contain a word. The search tool may require that (1) either the operator words themselves be typed in; (2) the operators be selected from a pull-down menu or checkbox; or (3) that "+" be used for "AND," or "–" for "NOT." If no operator is used between words, the rule normally followed is that documents containing both words are found first, followed by documents containing only one of the words (i.e., "AND" is assumed first, followed by "OR").

- *Give attention to the order of the keywords.* Some search indexes place greater emphasis on the word that appears first in a keyword phrase. It's best to order the keywords from the general to the particular. For example, "weather forecasting" is better than "forecasting weather" and "mammals plant eating" is better than "plant eating mammals."

- *Try synonyms.* I've already mentioned that at least one of the search indexes, Infoseek, will automatically search for synonyms, but you cannot count on any of them doing so reliably. Therefore, if your search is not turning up the kinds of documents you want, try repeating the search with synonyms. For example, try "automobiles" instead of "cars." Or you might want to use a more inclusive noun, such as "vehicles" or "transportation."

- *Avoid plurals and upper-case letters.* Normally, it's best to avoid using plurals and upper-case letters in your keywords because the singular, lower-case form represents the most general condition. That is, if your keywords are spelled in the singular form and lower case, most search tools will automatically find plural and upper-case forms also. The opposite is not necessarily true. Of course, there may be situations when you truly want to restrict your search to the plural and upper case. For example, you may want "automobile brakes," not "automobile brake," or you may want "Delta" the city in British Columbia, not the "delta" of a river.

Metasearching: Searching the Search Tools

At the risk of complicating matters by introducing yet another kind of search tool, this section would not be complete without mentioning the existence of metasearch tools. Metasearch tools are tools for searching search tools. This sounds like the epitome of bureaucracy—the creation of committees to study committees! In theory, metasearch tools offer the option of combining all search tools into one simple strategy to locate both Web and non-Web resources. You just enter your set of keywords once into a metasearch tool, and the tool searches a number of other tools and returns a list of what each individual tool found. In practice, metasearch tools don't work as smoothly as that because, as you've seen, there is considerable variation in the search language and search options used by each tool. Metasearch tools attempt to compensate for these differences as much as is practicable, but generally speaking, their results are not as reliable as those achieved using each tool separately. The frequent changes made to individual tools may confound metasearch tools, as well. Finally, metasearch tools tend to take longer than individual tools, although some tools allow you to set the maximum time permitted for the metasearch.

To get a listing of metasearch tools, go to Yahoo! and follow the path down from the top: *Computers and Internet: Internet: World Wide Web: Searching the Web: All-in-One Search Pages.* Three metasearch tools I recommend are:

- *MetaCrawler (http://metacrawler.cs.washington.edu).* This is technically the most sophisticated metasearch tool, and it is a delight to use. It searches nine of the major Web search indexes and offers the most flexibility in handling advanced searches of multiple indexes.

- *Internet Sleuth (http://www.isleuth.com).* Offering over fifteen hundred databases categorized by subject area, Internet Sleuth is one of the most comprehensive metasearch tools available. You can select two or more databases to be searched simultaneously within a given category of databases. Categories include Arts, Education, Government, Reference, Sports, and many others.

• *SEARCH.COM.* Strictly speaking, this service offered by CNET is not a metasearch tool like the others, since it cannot search multiple databases simultaneously. Instead, it's a collection of tools designed to find all kinds of information, Web sites, stock market quotes, phone numbers, software, and weather, to name just a few. You first select the category of information you want, select the tool you want to use, and enter your keywords into the form on SEARCH.COM's home page. There's even a tool that will allow a keyword search to determine which of its many databases is best for finding what you're looking for.

Part V

Ahead to Tomorrow

One exciting opportunity available now that will become even more widespread in the years to come is the chance to take professional-development courses over the Internet. Larry Winger, a mid-career scientist with a Ph.D., who lives in the far north of rural England, decided that he'd like to become a qualified teacher. Not wanting to leave his job to study full time, he decided to enroll in a distance education program supported and extended by the Internet and computer conferencing. Here is his story.

For a variety of reasons having to do with family, international moves, and innate stubbornness, I have not been able to find a permanent academic post, so my career, such as it is, has been a series of short-term postdoctoral contracts. I've taught undergraduates and students in master of science courses, as well as supervised and advised doctoral students. Recognizing that my age and experience were making me too expensive to be hired for contract work, and wanting to have a broader picture of science to help my daughter, who was entering secondary school, I decided I wanted to become a teacher.

While still working full time in research, I was privileged to be able to take advantage of a program offered in the UK and Europe by the Open University. The OU specializes in home-study courses, and had recently introduced a part-time Post-Graduate Certificate in Education (PGCE) course. The inception of this course was a result of a government move to promote the entry of people with suitable life experience into the teaching profession. Responding to an advertisement in one of our national newspapers, I joined the second cohort of students in this program, for the period of January 1995 to June 1996.

The PGCE course, which drew on the OU's wide experience in open and distance learning, consisted of intensive in-school training, assignments, face-to-face tutorial sessions, and a summative portfolio for final assessment. Printed course materials were supplemented by audio and video tapes. The course was enhanced by the use of First-Class conferencing software and the Internet, so that all participants, tutors, and subject specialists, as well as regional tutors and course directors, were linked in conferences. As I had become something of an Internet buff, I was able to draw upon a wide range of teaching material to share with my colleagues.

Professionally, I surprised myself by gaining a degree of confidence I had not expected. In simplest terms, I am now a qualified teacher, so that I am able to teach professionally in secondary science. I am certain that I could not have approached this training in any way other than as a participant in a part-time, computer-mediated course with the flexibility to continue my day job! The provision of the FirstClass network to all teacher-trainees and tutors meant that a support system was always there to deal with problems and to help expedite approaches to the lessons and teaching/learning theory. Moreover, home study in this way meant that, apart from the statutory setting of in-school training and the return of specific essays and reports, individual students could progress at their own rate.

My most serious problem in the course occurred during the final phase of in-school training, when I had some student discipline problems to contend with. Fortunately, with the prompt action of my regional tutor, as well as support both online and in tutorial sessions, I was able to develop an appropriate course of action and finish the program satisfactorily.

Although I am still employed in research for the short term, I take some satisfaction in the knowledge that I can and may teach science if circumstances change. If the opportunity arose for online courses through which I could develop marketable skills, I would certainly take advantage of them. So long as I am employed in my current position, I expect to be maintaining an unofficial OU PGCE alumni home page at *http://georgia.ncl.ac.uk/pgceal.html,* wherein links to the OU Education department, other testimonials, and a description of my partner school and local community, can be found.

14 | Where Are We Headed?

I began this book with a quotation from the late author Robertson Davies, who admonished us that if we give up the struggle to keep abreast of our ever changing world, we give up life. This is doubly true for the teaching profession! Not only do we as educators need to continually reflect on and improve our own teaching practice, we must bring to our classrooms the most up-to-date knowledge, ideas, and resources, with respect to both methodology and subject matter. In these pages, I urged you to take control of your professional development by devising a growth plan that includes concrete strategies for achieving your professional goals and objectives. My focus has been on how you can capitalize on the Internet to help you realize these aims.

As we head into the twenty-first century, the professional-development opportunities achievable with the Internet will be many times more profuse than today. Accompanying these opportunities will be new challenges. In this final chapter, I offer a glimpse into the future of professional development on the Internet.

Challenges We'll Face

All of us have witnessed the tremendous growth of the Internet since the mid-1990s, particularly since the advent of the Web. This growth will not only continue for the foreseeable future, but all signs indicate that it will accelerate. Estimates today suggest that in the time it takes you to read the next few paragraphs—about a minute—four to five new Web pages will have been created and twenty new users will be connected to the Internet!

Metcalfe's Law and the Future of the Internet

Not only will there simply be many, many more Web pages and an ever growing number of people using the Internet by century's end, but its "power," or what the network will literally be able to do, will increase dramatically as well. This prophecy is bolstered by what George Gilder, author of *Telecosm* (1996) calls Metcalfe's Law. Named after Robert Metcalfe, inventor of Ethernet, the world's most popular local area network, the law states that the potential power or value of a network is related to the square of the number of devices connected to it. To illustrate, consider how limited the usefulness of the telephone was initially because few people had phones. As more people began to get phones, the telephone system's value began to increase. With more and more telephone subscribers came increased services and features that would not have been possible or viable had there been only a few subscribers. Now, of course, the telephone system is an indispensable part of everyday life. According to Metcalfe's Law, the telephone's value did not just increase in direct proportion to the number of new subscribers, it increased exponentially as these new features, services, and uses became available. The same principle applies to any other networked system, be it roads, cable TV, or computers.

We are at the same stage with the Internet now as we were with the telephone system in its early days. A major difference is that the Internet is growing much faster than the telephone ever did. When we begin to consider the astounding growth rate of the Internet, coupled with the network's exponential increase in power predicted by Metcalfe's Law, even technology prophets become tongue-tied about what it will all mean over the next decade. One certainty is that the Internet will become a communications and information medium the likes of which we have never seen!

How Can We Cope with the Information Explosion?

As the Internet continues to grow unabated, a major challenge confronts us: How can we cope with the global sea of information available even now? Imagine that the next time you do a carefully constructed search on a set of relatively obscure keywords, your search engine reports that one hundred thousand entries *exactly* matched your keywords. How will you possibly make use of this search result? The first few pages of links won't necessarily provide you with the "best" links to the information, because there could be hundreds, if not thousands, of pages of equally relevant links. There is no simple answer to this question, but the scenario is very plausible. Here are some suggestions that can help you make the best of the overwhelming amount of information available on the Internet.

Don't Panic!   First, you have to realize that you won't be able to read everything about the topic you're researching. The days are gone when a single person is able to have a total grasp of all of the key concepts, developments, research, and writings in a particular field. The pace of advancement and dissemination of knowledge in most fields is so rapid today that being on top of your area of expertise one day is no guarantee that the next day you won't be overwhelmed by new material that appears out of nowhere. The reality is that the best you will likely be able to do is to understand the key trends and directions of knowledge development in your particular field, together with detailed knowledge about a few specific topics.

Stick to Your Plan   When exploring the Web, you've no doubt discovered how easy it is to stray off the topic you are inquiring about. You discover a link that's slightly off topic, yet interesting, so you decide to check it out quickly, with every intention of returning to where you left off. On the new page, you come upon yet another tempting link and click on it. Before long, you may have forgotten what you were originally looking for. I speak from my own experience when describing this all-too-common occurrence. My advice is to stick to your original research plan. Use Netscape's bookmark feature to mark sites that you may want to investigate later. You might even organize these bookmarks into a "To Do" bookmark folder in Netscape (see Chapter 3), then set aside some time periodically just to explore them. By doing this you'll ultimately make more productive use of your time, both achieving your research goals *and* satisfying your curiosity.

Keep Records of What You've Done   When I talked about setting up your professional-development action plan, you'll recall that I suggested that you keep what amounts to a travelogue—a record of where you have been on the Internet and what you've discovered. This is just another way to help you contend with the vast amount of information on the Internet. If you're the kind of person who shies away from keeping records, try to discipline yourself into keeping at least informal notes of the Web sites you've visited, including the topics you've searched and the search tools you've used. Tagging key Web sites with bookmarks will help, but remember to carefully organize and keep notes about these, lest you end up with an exceedingly long bookmark list of little value. Again, meaningful records are crucial time-savers.

Look for Summaries and Digests   Summaries and digests of research, provided they are credible and up-to-date, can be of great assistance to pursuing your professional-development goals. Often you don't need the kind of detail provided in primary-source documents (e.g., original research reports or articles) as when you are interested only in general trends and directions of a particular field. The ERIC digests mentioned in

Chapter 11 are one example of this type of document. When you read a digest, you are taking advantage of the expertise of selected authorities to gain insights into a specific field, insights that, had you to wade through the original research, would not be so readily attained. To locate articles that summarize or synthesize a field, try adding terms such as "summary," "synthesis," "abstract," or "digest" to your Internet keyword search string. One way to help ensure credibility of summaries is to look for those that are commissioned by reputable organizations such as professional associations, educational research institutions, and state and federal departments of education. Also, look for summaries published in refereed online journals (see Yahoo! for links to these) and work done by individuals who are well known in the field.

Seek Help From Virtual Professional Communities   We have seen how virtual professional communities enable networks of colleagues to share and discuss common concerns and interests. Virtual professional communities are an excellent source of advice and guidance when you are trying to track down information on a topic. When you post a request to a mailing list, hundreds if not thousands of professionals active in that field may read your request for help. Even if you get only a few replies, those replies may save you an inordinate amount of work trying to track down information on your own. I like to think of virtual professional communities as "distributed help networks." This is a term I've borrowed from computer network terminology, where distributed computing implies that the real power of a network lies with the individual workstations connected to it rather than with a central mainframe computer. Similarly, your colleagues probably hold more knowledge collectively than they do as individuals.

Evaluating Information

A major challenge inherent in the nature of the Internet—and compounded by its relentless expansion—is the difficulty of evaluating information. Information on the Internet appears disembodied and flat, often devoid of contextual clues to give you an idea of its worth. As I mentioned earlier, anyone can publish anything on the Internet. Documents rarely have the imprimatur of a publishing house, and only a small fraction of documents found on the Net are subjected to any kind of editorial or peer review. Some view this apparent chaos as a strength of the Internet, because the flow of information, ideas, and opinions is democratized. Others see it as a threat, because the established institutions that have traditionally interpreted, filtered, and controlled information are undermined. Regardless of where you may stand on this issue, in order to reap the most benefit from the Internet, you need to develop some techniques for gleaning the best of what is available.

You should realize that while all of the documents retrieved in a search may be equally *relevant* (in that your keywords occur as frequently in each document), there's a strong chance that they are not all equally *valuable*. Again, there are no easy answers to the question of how you can readily assess the value of documents you encounter. But there are some strategies you can use in evaluating Web documents or sites.

Make Use of Directories Containing Evaluated Web Sites   When doing research on a new field, I recommend you go to Web sites that contain directories or tools to search databases of evaluated Web sites. Many of the major companies hosting Web indexes and directories I talked about in Chapter 10 realize that the Internet community now wants to know more than just if a document exists—it also wants to know how good it is. Companies are now competing to see which one can distinguish itself with the best reviews of Web sites. Excite, Lycos, Magellan, and Yahoo! all contain large databases of Web site reviews. Two others you may wish to look at are CNET's Best of the Web (*http://www.cnet.com*) and NetGuide Live (*http://www.netguide.com*). Typically, these services employ professional reviewers to sift through the millions of Web pages to rate and categorize sites by topic.

While these best-of-the-Web services can be extremely helpful in separating the wheat from the chaff, you must realize that they vary considerably on dimensions such as:

- background and expertise of their reviewers
- coverage of topics and subject areas
- criteria for rating sites (some emphasize technical features more than others)
- scales for reporting the ratings (some use points, others stars)
- whether they can be easily searched, browsed, or both
- how often reviews are updated

Always check out the Help or About feature of these services to find out information of this kind before you use them. You will also want to browse the highest-rated sites in a field you're familiar with to get a feeling for the kind of site the service's reviewers consider exemplary.

Watch for Clues from the Site's URL   Judging a Web site by its URL is akin to judging a book by its cover, but in the absence of other information and when all sites appear to be equally relevant, you *can* get some clues about a site's potential value from its URL. Most search engines give the URLs of links in their list of search results. Directories don't usually provide the URLs of links; however, when you move the mouse pointer over any link, its URL will appear at the bottom of the window in Netscape.

You'll recall that the rightmost segment of a Web site's URL, known as its top-level domain, is determined by the kind of institution that hosts the site (e.g., *.com* is a commercial site and *.edu* is an American educational institution). Two-letter domains indicate a foreign country (e.g., *.au* is Australia and *.uk* is the United Kingdom). As a rule of thumb, I tend to look first at *.edu* and *.gov* (government) links when I have a long list of hits on a search of an academic or professional topic. If it's a topic about another country, I'll look for an educational institution's name appearing in a URL for that country. I tend to look last at links with *aol.com* (America Online) or *compuserve.com* (CompuServe), two popular Internet services, because these links will most likely be personal pages from the general public that typically give no contextual clues as to who the author is. In between my first and last choices I'll look at other *.com* sites, because they are less predictable: some commercial sites have excellent public resources, others are simply devoted to selling a product, while still others may be personal pages of customers of lesser-known Internet service providers. I will also consider *.org* and *.net* sites at this point because they may represent public institutions, libraries, and museums, but you should be aware that they could be special interest or lobbying groups that may have a strong bias in their materials.

There are no guarantees that using this strategy will yield the best information. Educational institutions, particularly universities, often do not put any restrictions on the quality or nature of content placed on their Web servers because of their regard for academic freedom. Also, be aware that students now frequently publish on university servers, so you are not necessarily getting the opinions of faculty when you go to university sites. Nor are you likely to find at *.gov* sites any documents critical of government policy. The reason I prefer *.edu* and *.gov* sites is because educational institutions are more likely to have links to an author's home page that may give you an indication of his or her credibility; at government sites you have access to official reports, public resources, statistics, and research documents that carry the imprint of the government.

Investigate Document Authors   Often you will come across a document that provides you with no indication of its author or how it relates to other documents at the site where you found it. This is because Web search engines index documents individually, without regard to how they relate to others at a particular site. You may find the ideas in the document interesting and relevant, but you will want some idea about who wrote it before deeming it credible. There is a strategy you can use to try to sleuth its author. It involves understanding how Web sites are typically structured. In Chapter 1, you saw that the URL of a Web site often consists of the address of the host computer followed by one or more forward slashes (/) with letters in between. This string of letters and slashes indicates the directory of the document at that Web site. Suppose you are viewing a document named *test.html* at the following URL:

http://www.heyu.edu/papers/test.html

You can strip off the document's name from the URL and enter into Netscape:

http://www.heyu.edu/papers/

This will take you to the default page for the directory */papers*. On this page, there's a chance you'll find clues as to who the document's author is or the context of the document. If you still don't get the information you need, try going up the directory path another level by removing segments of the URL to the right of the slash.

The Coming Bandwidth Squeeze

Some industry observers predict the imminent collapse of the Internet as it becomes overwhelmed by the sheer volume of traffic it supports. The problem is exacerbated not only by the influx of new users but by the growing demand for live audio and video and other kinds of multimedia services to be delivered over the Internet. These new services require high-bandwidth data-communications lines. The bandwidth of a data line is analogous to the pressure of water in a pipe. If all of the residents in a large number of homes connected to the same main water pipe opened their faucets full blast at the same time, the water pressure would drop for everybody. So too with the Internet; when a large number of users request multimedia data from servers across the Net, the data transmission speed on the main network lines slows to a crawl.

A major collapse has not yet happened, but undoubtedly you have experienced slowdowns when browsing the Web during peak business hours. These could be due to a bottleneck on the lines connecting Internet servers, the processing capacity of the server you're connecting to being exceeded, or a combination of both factors.

There is little you can personally do about the bandwidth squeeze, although you can try to schedule your online work during off-peak times if you continually experience bothersome slowdowns. Generally speaking, these times are from the wee hours of the morning until noon and on weekends. You may also want to consider switching to another Internet service provider. Most major commercial providers are constantly upgrading their communications lines to handle the ever rising demand for more bandwidth, but some companies are clearly ahead of others in this regard.

Fortunately, the bandwidth squeeze has not gone unnoticed by either the university research community or the federal government. A group of key universities, industry, and federal research agencies is working toward building the Next Generation Internet

(NGI). By early next century this network will allow data to flow a million times faster than today's home computer modems and one thousand times faster than the standard higher-speed T1 lines used by most universities and businesses. The goal of the NGI project is to create a network that will not only eliminate stagnation, but will allow people to work together over greater distances in new ways. It is especially geared toward the scientific community, as a facilitator of advanced research. Its developers foresee such things as enabling family doctors consulting live with specialists from around the globe, environmental researchers being able to model entire ecosystems, engineers developing products using virtual reality and simulation, schools and universities being able to deliver high-quality video courses on demand to remote sites, educators and others collaborating in shared virtual workspaces, and advanced instructional software being delivered online. Initially, about one hundred universities, research labs, and other institutions are being interconnected as a test bed network, although the intent is to make this newly developed technology rapidly available to the entire Internet community.

New Professional-Development Opportunities

Along with the challenges brought about by the explosion of information on the Internet come exciting professional-development opportunities. Some of these opportunities will be created by innovative tools that will allow us to do such things as collaborate in new kinds of virtual communities and explore virtual worlds. For the most part these tools will be incorporated into Web browsers as plug-ins or simply built into browsers as basic features. A broad range of Web-based courses will be available, addressing most teachers' professional-development needs. Other opportunities will be created at Web sites that offer services to help us with our research and keep us informed about topics of special interest. Here is a sampling of some of the new opportunities that will soon be widely available.

Brave New Collaborative Environments

In the discussion of virtual professional communities, you saw that mailing lists and newsgroups are the primary tools for the exchanging of ideas on the Internet. Although these tools will continue to be the mainstays for communication and collaboration over the Internet for some time, the trend is to move away from text-only communication toward richer environments that allow you to speak to others, see them, and share virtual workspaces. Many of these environments will make use of two powerful software tools, Sun Microsystems' Java programming language and Virtual Reality Modeling Language (VRML), which bring to life otherwise static Web pages and add depth to the two-dimensional computer screen. As you might expect, environments like these are predicated on high-bandwidth network connections.

You don't have to wait for these environments to be fully developed to get a sampling of what they will be like. Try visiting NASA's Jet Propulsion Lab (JPL) at *http://mpfwww.jpl.nasa.gov*. There you'll be able to drive an animated microrover across a realistic 3-D simulation of the surface of the planet Mars, just as JPL engineers navigate the real microrover from their headquarters in Pasadena. To do this, you need to download and install the free Cosmo Player plug-in for Netscape Navigator from *http://www.cosmo.com*. You can also view colorful virtual reality movies of the Mars surface using QuickTime VR, which is available free from *http://qtvr.quicktime.apple.com*. To take full advantage of this site you should have a direct Internet connection, although satisfactory results can be obtained with a high speed modem connection.

Another software application you may wish to look at to get an idea of how virtual environments are evolving is The Palace, found at *http://www.thepalace.com*. The Palace, which is starting to be used in schools, is a 3-D multimedia environment where you can chat and interact with anyone connected to the same Palace server. Unlike the tools mentioned above, The Palace functions very effectively over standard modem connections. When you connect to a server, you typically are taken to the entrance to a virtual building, which is made up of any number of virtual "rooms." Your presence in the building is represented by a "face" or "avatar," which you can edit to take on the appearance of any character you wish. When you want to talk to someone in the same room, you type your text at the bottom of the screen and it appears in a balloon beside your avatar. (A complete transcript of all of the conversations you hold is kept in a separate window.) Clicking with your mouse anywhere on your screen will take you to that part of the room. If you want to leave the room, you can click on a "hyperdoor," represented on the screen as a door in the room you're in, which then puts you into another room in the building.

Although The Palace is a stand-alone Internet software tool, it is closely linked to the Web. Most Palace servers have Web home pages, and Palace rooms contain links to Web pages. For example, a book lying on a table may represent a hyperlink to Web pages containing the book's content.

The Palace has an authoring language associated with it that allows servers to be created to represent any kind of virtual space imaginable—a school, a library, a town hall, a convention center, a store, an amusement park, a beach, or a ski resort. Because of this feature, together with its very low cost and visual appeal, we will no doubt soon see virtual communities constructed for teachers using The Palace, where they can gather to exchange ideas, talk to invited guests, and work together on projects.

Formal Online Courses

Across North America and, indeed, around the world, colleges and universities are increasingly seeing the Internet as a medium for delivering courses to a wider range of students than they could normally reach. Two early starters in this field were the Open University and Birkbeck College, both in England, which began experimenting with Internet-based instruction for off-campus as early as 1994. Now they are joined by a host of other institutions offering both credit and noncredit courses. Three kinds of institutions offer online courses: (1) traditional colleges and universities that provide electronic versions of their regular course offerings supplemented by new courses tailored to the Internet community, (2) established distance-education institutions that are converting traditional correspondence courses to Web-based versions, and (3) new "cyber universities," some of which are not yet accredited, that are springing up to offer online courses exclusively. All three types of institutions currently offer both undergraduate and graduate courses—some even offer entire degree programs via the Internet. There is no doubt that over the next few years both the number and variety of courses offered online will increase dramatically. To obtain a listing of institutions offering online courses, follow the path at Yahoo! *Education: Distance Learning: Colleges and Universities.*

What's an Online Course Like?   Typically, online courses are offered using common generic Internet tools. For example, you'll register by completing a form at the institution's home page on the Web. Then you'll likely be provided with an ID and password to access the course's home page. On this page you'll find the course syllabus, links to online course readings and related resources, and possibly online tutorials containing video clips and animated illustrations of key concepts. Web-based conferencing or a chat facility may also be attached to the course, fostering discussion about course content with instructors and other students. Other courses may provide you with access to a specialized conferencing tool for this purpose, such as FirstClass or Lotus Notes; or you may simply be provided an e-mail address to maintain contact with the instructor and subscribe to a class mailing list.

Exciting new tools are being developed specifically for online courses. These tools are built around a pedagogical philosophy that views students as active learners who construct their own understanding of the topic at hand, rather than as passive recipients of the instructor's knowledge. Students are given opportunities to collaborate with others in the course on problem-solving projects or virtual labs, they participate in virtual seminars, and they conduct individual research projects. Instructors are present online to act as mentors and to guide students in achieving desired goals.

One outstanding example of this type of tool is Virtual-U, now under development at the TeleLearning Network of Centers of Excellence at Simon Fraser University in

British Columbia. When you enter Virtual-U, you see the 3-D representation of its "campus." This unique campus features the same buildings you would see on any campus, including academic and administration buildings, a library, and a student center (called the virtual café). Clicking on any building will bring you inside, where you might find 3-D spaces for navigating to a specific room in which you can collaborate with others, meet the instructor, conduct experiments, access resources, and even register for courses without having to wait in line!

Would You Want to Take an Online Course?   Much debate is taking place in the halls of academia today on the merit of online courses. As you would expect, the debate ranges from one extreme—the view that online courses are fraudulent ways for institutions to save money—to the other—the view that such courses offer a superior alternative to the overcrowded lecture hall all too common in institutions of higher learning. While most students enrolled in online courses say that they miss the face-to-face contact with the instructor and fellow students found in traditional programs, they frequently find the experience rewarding and report that they learn more in online courses than in traditional ones for various reasons. For instance, students who are reluctant to speak in regular classes find that they can express their ideas without intimidation when working online. The ability to work whenever you want and from the comfort of your home are added attractions. A final benefit of online courses is that you are not disadvantaged when your local college or university does not offer courses on the topic you want, because online courses can be taken from institutions anywhere in the world.

The Agents are Coming, the Agents are Coming

Imagine having a personal assistant who, knowing the goals of your professional-development action plan, roamed the Internet to locate relevant Web sites, resources, courses, and upcoming events to help you reach your goals. Now imagine that this assistant was a piece of software. Far-fetched? No, it isn't. Intelligent software assistants—called agents—now exist that accomplish some of these tasks. What's more, developments are under way to produce agents that will transform the very way we interact with the Web in the not too distant future. For example, there are now projects in progress aimed at having agents do the following tasks:

• *Retrieve information.* Agents will be given their owners' information preferences—be it news on a specific topic, research reports, government press releases, or literally any other kind of information found on the Web—and then they will continually travel the Web gathering information for their owners. As the agents bring back information, they will learn from their owners whether the retrieved information matches their interests and, if not, modify their search criteria accordingly.

- *Conduct online commerce.* Agents will be able to do comparison shopping for consumer products on the Web, make travel reservations, purchase insurance, seek employment opportunities for their owners, and act as real-estate brokers. Your agent will even be able to negotiate business deals with other agents and handle the necessary financial transactions.

- *Meet others.* People will be able to provide their agents with a profile of their personal or professional interests, and then send the agent out onto the Web searching for agents of other people having matching profiles. Once the agents determine that the profiles match, their owners would be notified and they could arrange to contact one another.

- *Act on behalf of a community.* Agents need not work only for individuals. There are projects under way in which agents determine a community's common interests and then search for Web pages that match members' collective preferences.

Much research and development still needs to be done before agents become the accepted way of conducting Internet business. Two technical roadblocks now preventing greater use are the lack of agreed-upon standards for the conducting of commerce through agents, and the need to establish guidelines for ethical agent behavior. When visiting servers, for instance, agents must be able to identify themselves and obey the wishes of the server. Moreover, they must be responsive to their owners, as even one out-of-control agent could wreak havoc on the Internet. Finally, people must feel comfortable using them. Agents will have the capacity to initiate action without explicit guidance from their owners. People may find this kind of autonomous behavior difficult to accept in a machine.

You can try out a prototype agent called BargainFinder at Andersen Consulting's Web site. (At the time of writing, the URL was *http://bf.cstar.ac.com/bf/*. BargainFinder is an experimental project, however, so you may need to use a search engine to locate it.) BargainFinder accomplishes a relatively simple task—searching for the best buy on popular CD albums on the Web. Nevertheless, it demonstrates the enormous promise of agents, and their potential impact on the marketplace. The developers chose to demonstrate BargainFinder with CD shopping because CDs are a well-known and cataloged commodity sold on the Web.

Here's what a typical "shopping trip" with BargainFinder looks like. First, you enter in the artist and title of the CD you're interested in, as illustrated in Figure 14–1. Once you click on *Shop for the album*, off goes BargainFinder to do some comparison shopping by visiting up to nine online music stores, while you sit back and relax. After a minute or two, BargainFinder returns with a list of prices and stores that have the requested CD. When I did this, I found considerable variation among the stores in the CD's cost.

Figure 14–1

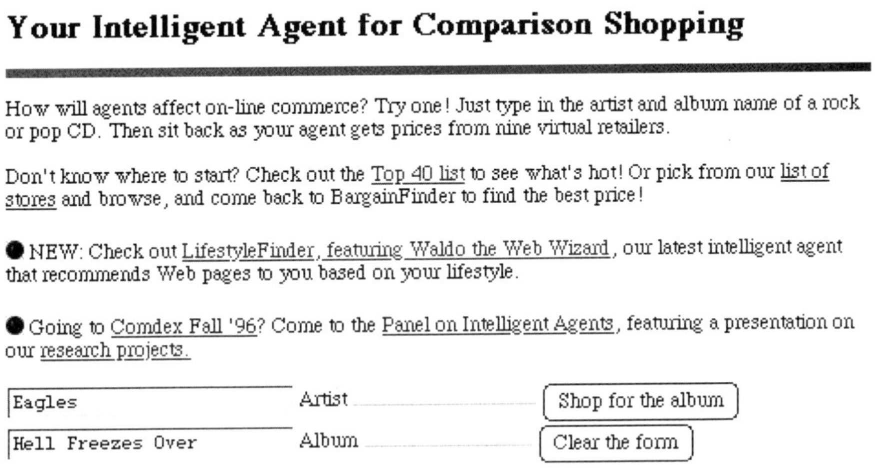

Your Intelligent Agent for Comparison Shopping

How will agents affect on-line commerce? Try one! Just type in the artist and album name of a rock or pop CD. Then sit back as your agent gets prices from nine virtual retailers.

Don't know where to start? Check out the Top 40 list to see what's hot! Or pick from our list of stores and browse, and come back to BargainFinder to find the best price!

● NEW: Check out LifestyleFinder, featuring Waldo the Web Wizard, our latest intelligent agent that recommends Web pages to you based on your lifestyle.

● Going to Comdex Fall '96? Come to the Panel on Intelligent Agents, featuring a presentation on our research projects.

| Eagles | Artist | Shop for the album |
| Hell Freezes Over | Album | Clear the form |

Some stores were blocking BargainFinder when I carried out my search. These merchants apparently were not happy with consumers shopping via an agent. Were their prices higher, perhaps? Did they resent not having consumers visit their store directly to see their advertising? One can only speculate as to why they blocked BargainFinder, but merchants who ignore the coming wave of agent-assisted shopping will do so at their peril.

Agents may seem like the stuff of science fiction writers today, but some analysts predict that agent traffic will one day surpass human-initiated traffic over the Internet. Though this technology is still largely in the experimental stage, it may soon play an indispensable role in professional development on the Internet.

A Final Word

As we move into the next century, no one knows the extent to which the Internet will grow or exactly how it will evolve. One certainty, however, is that the Internet will become a significantly larger part of our everyday life and exceedingly richer in content and utility.

Major challenges include dealing with the extremely rapid increase in information available on the Internet, and determining the merit of information you uncover. Another challenge we collectively must deal with is the tremendous pressure we are putting on the existing information infrastructure as we demand more bandwidth for new kinds of services. Some of your major professional-development opportunities of the future will be to communicate and work with colleagues in 3-D multimedia online environments, to enroll in any one of an exceedingly wide selection of continuing- and graduate-education courses offered over the Internet, and to use software agents to assist you in tracking down information and carrying out various tasks.

Now that you've seen how the Internet can help you grow professionally today, and how it will be an increasingly valuable tool for your development in the future, the time to begin your action plan is right away. Start by writing down a list of the knowledge and skills you want to achieve, and then devise a strategy linked to the Internet to accomplish them. Don't wait until you have a large block of time to begin this process. By working only several hours a week, you'll be surprised at how much you can accomplish. Not only will the process be professionally rewarding, I'm certain that you will find using the Internet to realize your goals thoroughly fascinating and enjoyable. I invite you to share your experiences with me and other readers at this book's Web site at *http://www.edu.yorku.ca/MTL*.

Appendix: Further Readings

Further information about any of the topics discussed in this book can be found on the Internet. Printed resource lists of URLs, however, are typically outdated even before they are published because of the fast-changing nature of the Net. Since the emphasis of this book has been to help you develop Internet research skills, rather than providing you with a list of resources, I suggest you turn to Yahoo! (*http://www.yahoo.com*) to locate additional readings.

Below is a list of topics, and the path at Yahoo! where you can find more information on them. Even though you may only see one entry beside a topic, in most cases, there are many, many links to sites related to the topic. To follow a path such as *Top: Computers and Internet: Internet: History*, you should go to the home page of Yahoo! (called the Top), click on the link *Computers and the Internet*, click on *Internet*, and finally click on *History* to see a listing of resources on the topic. If the directory structure of Yahoo! changes, and the paths below are no longer valid, you needn't worry. Simply search Yahoo! using several of the words from the path as keywords and you're almost certain to find helpful resources.

Chapter 1: What Do I Need to Know About the Internet?

Topic	*Yahoo! Path*
History	Top: Computers and Internet: Internet: History
Basic concepts, protocols, URLs, clients and servers	Top: Computers and Internet: Internet: Information and Documentation

Topic	Yahoo! Path
	see also
	Top: Computers and Internet: Internet: World Wide Web: FAQs
How to use the Internet	Top: Computers and Internet: Internet: Information and Documentation: Beginner's Guides

Chapter 2: Making the Most of Your Electronic Mail

Topic	Yahoo! Path
E-mail software reviews, links to software home pages	Top: Computers and Internet: Software: Reviews: Individual: Internet: Email
Appropriate use of e-mail and other forms of electronic communication	Top: Computers and Internet: Internet: Information and Documentation: Beginner's Guides: Netiquette

Chapter 3: Accessing Internet Resources with a Web Browser

Topic	Yahoo! Path
Browsers, helpers, plug-ins, comparisons of browsers, links to browser home pages	Top: Computers and Internet: Software: Internet: World Wide Web: Browsers

Chapter 4: How to Develop an Action Plan

Topic	Yahoo! Path
Professional-development planning, related activities, sites	Top: Education and then search on the keywords "professional development"

Chapter 5: Virtual Communities and Professional Development

Topic	Yahoo! Path
Basic concepts of virtual communities	Top: Education: Online Forums

Topic	Yahoo! Path
	see also
	Top: Society and Culture: Cyberculture
	and
	Top: Arts: Humanities: Philosophy: Philosophers: Rheingold, Howard

Chapter 6: Community Mailing Lists

Topic	Yahoo! Path
Available lists, user guides, search tools, archives	Top: Computers and Internet: Internet: Mailing Lists
	see also
	Top: Education: Online Forums: Mailing Lists

Chapter 7: Newsgroups

Topic	Yahoo! Path
Frequently asked questions (FAQs) about newsgroups	Top: Reference: FAQs: Usenet
	see also
	Top: News and Media: Usenet
Links to newsgroup that post FAQs	Top: Computers and Internet: Software: Internet: Usenet: FAQs
Newsgroup software	Top: Computers and Internet: Software: Internet: Usenet
Education newsgroup links	Top: Education: Usenet

Chapter 8: Other Kinds of Virtual Professional Communities

Topic	Yahoo! Path
Computer conferencing software	Top: Computers and Internet: Software: Communications and Networking: Groupware
Links to IRC sites	Top: Education: Online Forums: Chat
Educational MOO links	Top: Education: Instructional Technology: On-line Teaching and Learning: Educational MOOs

Topic	Yahoo! Path
Videoconferencing software	Top: Computers and Internet: Multimedia: Videoconferencing

Chapter 9: Why Use the Internet for Your Research? and Chapter 10: Finding Information on the Web

Topic	Yahoo! Path
Tools and techniques for Web searching	Top: Computers and Internet: Internet: Searching the Net
	see also
	Top: Computers and Internet: Internet: World Wide Web: Searching the Web
Links to search engines	Top: Computers and Internet: Internet: World Wide Web: Searching the Web: Search Engines
Links to directories	Top: Computers and Internet: Internet: World Wide Web: Searching the Web: Web Directories

Chapter 11: Searching Bibliographic Databases

Topic	Yahoo! Path
Links to home pages of libraries of the world and related information	Top: Reference: Libraries

Chapter 12: Finding Other Kinds of Information on the Internet

Topic	Yahoo! Path
Searching for FTP resources	Top: Computers and Internet: Internet: FTP Sites: Searching
Searching for Gopher resources	Top: Computers and Internet: Internet: Gopher: Searching
Searching for newsgroup resources	Top: News and Media: Usenet: Searching and Filtering

Chapter 13: Devising an Internet Research Strategy

Topic	Yahoo! Path
Comparisons of Web search engines	Top: Computers and Internet: Internet: World Wide Web: Searching the Web: Comparing Search Engines

Chapter 14: Where Are We Headed?

Topic	Yahoo! Path
Future of Internet	Top: Computers and Internet: Internet: Statistics and Demographics
New collaborative environments	Top: Computers and Internet: Internet: World Wide Web: Virtual Reality Modeling Language (VRML)
	see also
	Top: Recreation: Games: Internet Games: Virtual Worlds: 3D Worlds
Online courses	Top: Education: Distance Learning: Colleges and Universities
Intelligent agents	Top: Science: Computer Science: Artificial Intelligence: Machine Learning: Intelligent Software Agents

Index